QUIRKY GIRL

THE FLYNNS BOOK SIX

KAYT MILLER

Copyright © 2020 by Kayt Miller

All rights reserved.

No part of this book may be reproduced in any form or by any electronic or mechanical means, including information storage and retrieval systems, without written permission from the author, except for the use of brief quotations in a book review.

 Created with Vellum

THE FLYNN FAMILY

--- 6 ---

QUIRKY GIRL

CONTENTS

Chapter 1	1
Chapter 2	9
Chapter 3	15
Chapter 4	21
Chapter 5	31
Chapter 6	37
Chapter 7	49
Chapter 8	63
Chapter 9	67
Chapter 10	77
Chapter 11	81
Chapter 12	91
Chapter 13	97
Chapter 14	107
Chapter 15	109
Chapter 16	115
Chapter 17	121
Chapter 18	125
Chapter 19	127
Chapter 20	135
Chapter 21	139
Chapter 22	141
Chapter 23	145
Chapter 24	153
Chapter 25	159
Chapter 26	167
Chapter 27	173
Chapter 28	175
Chapter 29	179
Chapter 30	185
Chapter 31	189

Chapter 32	193
Chapter 33	197
Chapter 34	201
Epilogue	207
Books by Kayt Miller	211
Acknowledgments	213
About the Author	217
Thank you!	219
Sneak Peek: FarmBoy	221

CHAPTER ONE

ED: MY LITTLE BROTHERS WEDDING

Just thirty more minutes and I can get out of here. When I'm done with my big-brother duties, I'm free to go home, drink a beer, and watch baseball or something mindless that requires no effort on my part to enjoy.

All in all, the wedding turned out pretty good. My speech at the beginning of the reception was short and sweet—emphasis on short. Everyone has eaten, had cake, and now they're on the "get drunk and dance" portion of the night, and that scene is not for me.

From my spot in a dark corner of the ballroom, I can observe everything that's happening around me. Ethan and Claire had their ceremony and reception in the same room—not a bad idea, really. If I were to ever marry, I'd do something like this. I scoff aloud. *Who the hell am I kidding?* I'll never get married. Too much can go wrong with a marriage or, fuck, even a relationship. Not only do 50 percent of marriages end in divorce, a bunch more end when one of the pair keels over. No thanks. The odds for a long, happy marriage are definitely not in my favor. I'm so sure of these facts that I haven't even dated anyone seriously. Ever. I've had a few short-term flings, sure, and my share of one-night stands, but nothing serious. I can't risk it. Too many people count on me. I need to keep my head on straight.

With a sigh, I look around the room again. So far, no one has punched anyone else, and I've seen no catfights or other signs that things are getting out of hand. That doesn't mean there won't be, because there's about a 100 percent chance one or more of the Flynns will do something to turn this nice reception into a barroom brawl. I blame the Irish in all of us—it's inevitable.

I scan the room again, looking for my dad. When I spot him sitting at a table with his brother, Declan, our eyes meet. He smiles and nods at me, and I do the same. Dad knows me better than anyone. He gets I'm a loner and that I hate shit like this, so when it's time for my Irish goodbye, he won't be surprised I'm gone. It won't bother anyone else either—no, they won't care. With the wedding done, my role as my baby brother's watchdog and protector is essentially over. Now that Ethan is a married man, he's on his own. Next will be Ernie, my middle brother. That's a shock to my system. I never thought Ernie would settle down. And the woman he fell for is so far removed from his usual bimbos. Kennedy Corcoran is a great girl—smart, funny, tough as nails, and not afraid of anything. Maybe that's why it works. She doesn't put up with Ernie's shit.

I'm momentarily distracted when the song changes to an M.C. Hammer song, and I watch Claire, my new sister-in-law, take a swing at Ernie. His head is thrown back in a laugh. Ethan looks pissed, and Kennedy seems confused. I'd say Claire was teasing, but she just made contact with Ernie's shoulder, and it looks like it was hard enough to knock the big oaf off balance. He caught himself before he fell. Her anger doesn't stop him from wrapping his arms around the new Mrs. Flynn in a hug. Crisis averted. It looks like the newest Flynn has a good right hook. Noted.

CHAPTER 1

Shifting my gaze to the left, I check out the bar. There's a line of about fifteen people waiting to get their free drinks thanks to the open bar. I pick up my glass of Guinness and sip. I'm only having the one drink. I need a clear head. Why? No reason. I just like to be in control in case someone needs me. Glancing further right, I spot the waitress that keeps grabbing my attention—mind you, not for a good reason. This girl should *not* be waiting tables. I've watched her elbow Aunt Marge, my mom's sister, in the arm and press her boobs, what there is of them, into the side of my cousin Mick's head as she reached for his empty glass. She's broken at least one glass and a plate, and she's not even gotten to this side of the room yet.

Her hair is... I'm not even sure I can describe it accurately. It's blondish. I guess you could call it dirty, strawberry blonde. There seem to be different colors of blonde, red, and brown running through it, but that's not the part that stands out. It's the fact that she's got it wadded up into a ball on the top of her head and pieces are sticking out all over the place that draws my attention. Some pieces are sticking straight up, some in her eyes, and others are pointing out on either side of her head. It's like she fixed her hair and then found herself in a category four hurricane on the way to work and left it that way.

Scanning her body from head to toe, I wince. Her uniform is tight. It's way too small for a girl with her kind of body. She's all ass and thighs. The black skirt she's wearing barely covers her round bottom. She's paired the skirt with a blouse that's at least two sizes too small. Then, she's wrapped up the entire thing with white knee-high socks, like the ones Catholic girls wear, and dark Converse tennis shoes. Ordinarily, I'd say that look is hot, but not on this girl. Not tonight.

When she turns in my direction, I get a look at her face. It's pretty—at least the parts that aren't covered by hunks of loose hair. I can see one big eye and a cute little nose, as well as full lips that she's painted bright pink. As she approaches my table, I lean back into the shadows. She's picking up plates, silverware, and water glasses and piling them on top of each other. It's too much to carry all at once. When she lifts the pile, several pieces of silver slide off the top and onto the floor.

"Shoot!" she hisses. Setting down the things in her arms, she turns away from me and bends down to pick them up.

I blink twice as she bends over because her skirt rises up and up and up until I see most of her Wonder Woman underwear. The panties are blue with white stars all over them, and smack dab in the center of her ass is the Wonder Woman logo. I let out a snort of a laugh, which startles her. The forks, spoons, and knives she's holding fly into the air and scatter around her. When she turns in my direction, I say, "You're not very good at this, are you?"

"Huh?" She blinks her long eyelashes at me.

"Waitressing. You're not good at it."

"Uh, I, uh, I don't know."

"Well, I can tell you, you *aren't*."

Her chin begins to quiver, and then she licks those full lips and bites her bottom one. Sniffling, she lets out a sob. "It's.... I'm not bad at it. It's just—" She sniffles again. "—it's the anniversary of Mr. Nibblesworth's death."

"Mr. Nibblesworth?" Who the fuck is Mr. Nibblesworth?

She sobs louder. "My c-c-cat. Mr. Barnabus Nibblesworth. He d-d-died s-s-six months ago t-t-today. I c-can't concentrate. All I can do is th-th-think about my big, fuzzy buddy. Oh, God...." Her sobs turn into a full-on crying jag in a matter of seconds. She leaves everything on the table and floor and runs away, weaving in and out of the sea of round banquet tables, tripping and nearly falling at one point.

"Shit." I rise to my feet and follow her, muttering, "Not my finest hour making the weird waitress cry." When I find her,

CHAPTER 1

she's still sobbing as she puts dirty dishes into one of those plastic bins that go back to the dishwashing area. I clear my throat. Not knowing what to say, I go with, "Uh, miss? I'm sorry... about your cat." However, I'm *not* sorry I pointed out her obvious lack of waitressing skills. Someone needed to tell her.

She whirls around like a tornado and throws her arms around my neck. "Oh, you're so sweet. I'm the one that's sorry. I'm a blubbering crybaby. I was trying *soooo* hard not to cry tonight."

Feeling the back of my shirt grow wet, I glance over my shoulder and see a wine glass perched on my shoulder. A wine glass that's in her hand and one that's now facing downward—remnants of red wine still in the glass. I look back at her expecting her to say something like, "Oops. Sorry about spilling wine down your back." But she says nothing. I look back over my shoulder and can only imagine what I must look like. Like I've just been murdered.

"Look, I'm sorry about your, uh, loss."

She presses her face into my neck, and several strands of her unruly hair end up in my mouth. I feel her head nod up and down, and the scent of her hair finds its way into my nostrils. Sweet and tropical. Coconut? Not only that. I believe I feel hard nipples pressing into my chest.

"You're so nice," she says as she pulls away from me. With her hands now resting on my chest, she looks up at me, smiles, and blinks rapidly. "Wow, you're really good-looking."

"Uh, thanks?" I look down at her and can't help noticing her shirt is gaping open at the top. I do my best not to stare, but I can't help it. I'm a guy, and there are nipples in my line of sight.

"Not as good-looking as the groom, though. He's a fox."

I blink and look at her questioningly. "A fox?" She thinks Ethan is a fox?

"Yeah, and the other guy in the tuxedo, he's hotter than you too. But you're very good-looking."

Ernie. She's talking about Ernie now. "Great. Thanks." Jesus, was that supposed to be a compliment? I look down her shirt again. I can't help it. Jesus, I haven't seen a chest that flat since I accidentally saw Karen McCormick's boobs in sixth grade. She dove into the pool, and when she came up for air, she was topless. I recall at the time being quite aroused at the sight, but these bee stings, not so much.

"Eyes up here, please," she says, pointing to her face. She's got a smirk on her lips like she thinks she caught me stealing a peek. It was an accident, believe me. "My name's Beatrice, but I mostly go by Bea, so, yeah." She pauses. "What's your name?"

Her eyes are glistening with unshed tears. "Uh, Ed."

"Ed? Not Edward? Eddie? Ooh, I know, *Eduuuaaarrrdddooo*. That's sexy. You should definitely go by Eduardo."

"No. It's just Ed."

"Do you like dolphins, Eduardo?"

"Dolphins?" Wow, she changes subjects fast.

"Yeah. Do. You. Like. Dolphins?" she says, rolling her eyes like I'm the idiot here.

"I guess."

"Well, I *looovvveee* dolphins. Have you ever been to Shedd Aquarium?"

"When I was twelve."

"Well, I *love* Shedd Aquarium. I try to go as often as possible. They have this dolphin show there that is Out. Of. This. World. If I could get a do-over, I'd totally become a dolphin trainer."

Once she's finished with that speech, I reach up and pull her hands away from my chest. "Well, since you seem to be okay, I'd better get back...."

"Give me your phone."

"Excuse me?"

"Give me your phone," she says, holding her palm out to me.

I have no idea why I do it, but I pull it out of my back pocket and hand it to her. I watch her program her number into my phone and then send herself a text. Great. She's got my number.

"Okay, I'm going to call you later."

"Why?"

"To set up a time to meet."

"Meet?"

"At Shedd. Duh!"

"I don't—"

"If you haven't been there since you were twelve, you're going to be b-l-o-w-n, blown away by it now. It's so amazing." She turns to walk around me. "Okay. Talk to you later," she says, waving her pink-tipped fingernails at me.

As I watch her go, I mutter, "What the fuck just happened?"

FLOPPING DOWN ONTO MY COUCH, I grab the remote for my television. Finally. I'm home. I was able to sneak out of the reception without anyone seeing me. Well, someone probably saw me, but they didn't try and stop me. My family knows me.

"Let's see what's on tonight." Raising my legs, I rest them on my reclaimed wood coffee table and take a pull of my beer. Now, I can finally relax after a long day of family shit—not that I mind my family shit. I don't. I love my dad and my brothers. It just gets to be overwhelming sometimes. The fact that I need to watch out for them twenty-four seven takes its toll. I rest my head on the back of my couch and change the TV to one of my favorite movies. I've seen it so many times over the years; I could probably recite the dialogue verbatim. Changing my mind, I press a few buttons on the remote in search of a baseball game.

Just as I'm about to tune into a Cubs game, my phone rings. I groan loudly as I reach in front of me to pick up my phone from the coffee table. I don't recognize the number, but I answer it anyway. "Hello."

"Eduardo?"

I pause. Maybe if I pretend I'm not here, she'll go away.

"Eduardo?"

"It's Ed."

"Eduardo? It's me, Beatrice. Remember? We met at that hot guy's wedding."

"It was two hours ago. Of course I remember."

Maybe she doesn't understand sarcasm because she just ignores my comment, saying, "So, I was just calling to get our ducks in a row about tomorrow."

"Tomorrow?" *Ducks in a row?* Who says that shit?

Paying no attention to my question, she keeps going. "Let's meet promptly at nine o'clock outside next to the fountain with the man holding the fish. I'll wear a flower in my hair, so you can recognize me. Okay? Don't be late! Sunday's are a nightmare at Shedd. Okay, bye!" she says in an overly happy and annoyingly chipper voice.

I don't get a chance to reply because she's already gone. "Hello?" I hold my phone out in front of my face and stare at it, wishing that last two minutes didn't happen. "I'm not going to damn Shedd Aquarium with a girl who's obviously got a screw loose." I should just call her back. But then what? She'd just ramble on and on, not paying one bit of attention to what I'm saying. "Aw, hell. I don't have time for this." I toss the phone back onto the table and let my head drop onto the back of my sofa with a groan. "Once. I'll play along once. After that, I'm abso-fucking-lutely shaking this chick off." Definitely. Letting her loose.

CHAPTER TWO

ED

At a quarter to ten the next morning, I pull my phone out of my back pocket to check the time. Again. "Nine o'clock, my ass." I look up from my phone and blink. I blink again just to be sure I'm not hallucinating. I know it's her. Who else would it be in that getup? "What the fuck is she wearing?" I mumble. As she moves closer, I slowly remove my sunglasses, so I can take in the entire ensemble unfiltered. Her feet—I'll start there. They're covered in Converse sneakers. One blue. One red. Moving upward, I can't see any skin as it's hidden behind a layer of skirt that's almost hitting the ground as it trails behind her. Oh wait, the skirt is sort of sheer, so I do get a glimpse of her legs beneath the fabric—fabric with a pattern that reminds me of an ancient quilt my grandma used to have. A seriously ugly quilt.

I note the fact that the skirt is flowing at the bottom, but it seems to hug her thighs and hips. Not a surprise, she's bottom heavy for sure. At ten yards away, I let my eyes move upward. Her top half is covered by a tiny white tee shirt. It's so tight I can almost make out the tiny bumps of her breasts that would be better suited on a prepubescent girl—or boy. The image on the front of the tee catches my eye. I can see the logo for Shedd Aquarium. As she moves closer, I make out the word: *Harry Otter*. At five yards, I can just make out the face of a cartoon seal or, I guess, it's an otter wearing robes like they wore in Harry Potter. The otter's got on round glasses, and it's holding a wand. "Harry Otter." Now, I might think that was funny if someone else—anyone else—was wearing it, but I'm not laughing because this girl is weird as fuck, and that's no joke.

As she gets close, I look up at her face. *Whoa.* She's pretty. Beautiful. It doesn't look like she's wearing much makeup. Her freckles are clear as day out here. Her lips are pink like last night. I thought she was wearing lipstick at the reception, but now I'm not so sure. They almost look like they're naturally that perfect shade of pink. Her hair is down today. It's long and wild like I figured it'd be after seeing it last night. But when the sun hits it, the blonde and strawberry blonde highlights practically shine. She's got braids here and there and a bunch of white daisies in her hair. I see a black and white earring peeking out near her cheek—yin and yang symbols. Damn, she looks like she belongs at Woodstock, circa 1969.

Stopping right in front of me, she looks up and says excitedly, "You made it!"

I made it? I've been fucking sitting on this brick wall for forty-five—no, fifty minutes. "Uh, yeah. You're late."

She giggles. "Oh, I know. Traffic was cray-cray. The bus took forever."

"The bus? You took the bus? Where do you live?"

"Albany Park."

Albany Park? I live in the Cragin neighborhood, just southeast of her. It took me forty minutes by car. The bus would take significantly longer. "That's way up there. Why didn't you drive?"

"Oh, I don't drive."

CHAPTER 2

"You don't have a car?"

"Oh, I've got a car. I just don't drive. I take the bus or ride my bike."

Okay. Why do I get the feeling this conversation is going nowhere? Besides, I don't really give two shits why she, a grown-ass woman, doesn't drive. Once this date is over, I'll never see her again. Date? Did I just call this a date? *Not a date.* Time to move on. "So, are we doing this thing?" I ask, pointing to the admissions entrance.

"Oh, yes!" she says, jumping up and down and clapping her hands. "Oh, dang. There's a line."

"Great." Now I get to stand in line with her. Nightmare.

As sure as the sun sets, the minute we get into line, this chick starts jabbering on and on about dolphins. "Eduardo? Did you know that there are nearly forty species of dolphins?"

I look down at her and blink. Am I supposed to answer that? From the look on her face and the fact she's staring up at me blinking frantically, I think that's a yes. "No."

"Well, there are. Also, dolphins are carnivores. Not that surprising, I guess. I bet you already knew they didn't live on seaweed." She snorts with laughter.

I look up to the front of the line and wish to the heavens above that the fifty people in front of me would suddenly decide to leave.

"Dolphins are part of the family of whales that include orcas and pilot whales." I pull my phone out and check the time. Ten after ten. "Are you even listening to me?"

Nodding, I say, "Orcas." Being the oldest of three boys, I learned a long time ago how to multitask. I can do all sorts of things while also keeping an eye or, in this case, an ear out for the little terrors born after me.

"Right. Well, did you know that dolphins have acute

eyesight and can hear frequencies ten times that of an adult human?"

"Wow," I deadpan. That seems to be all I need to say since she keeps right on going. We've moved three steps since she started rambling on about dolphins. I look down at her and can't help noticing how animated she is. Damn, she *really* loves dolphins.

"What do you think is the dolphin's main threat in the wild?"

"Humans."

She gasps, and her eyes grow to double their size. "Yes!" she squeals and claps again. "How did you know that? Almost everyone thinks it's sharks."

Shrugging, I mutter, "Hmm, fascinating." Yeah, sarcasm. Deal with it. I look up and see the line moving faster as a large group moves over to the left out of the line. I place my palm on her back to nudge her forward. A shiver runs up my arm at the contact. She must have shocked me. No doubt her swishing skirt created the energy to generate the static charge.

We're close enough to the entrance that I can see the cashiers in their cubicles taking money. "So, I was thinking... we *have* to see the dolphin show."

"Uh-huh."

"Also, I think you'd get a kick out of the penguins."

"Uh-huh."

"Great!" she says excitedly. Turning to face me, she wraps her arms around my neck. Up on her tiptoes, she presses her lips to my face before I can push her away. She kisses my cheek three times and says, "This is going to be so awesome."

Sure, I should have pushed her away, but what harm did it do? Besides, it felt kind of nice.

When we finally make it up to the ticket counter, I let the little nerd take the lead. "Yes, we need two general admission tickets, Chicago residents. Plus, we want to see the dolphin show and," she says, peeking back at me, "we want to do the Extraordinary Experience. Penguins."

"Great," says the ticket person. "That'll be $228.50."

I stand still, staring at the ticket person. I feel eyes on me, so I look down and see, oh, shit, what the hell's her name? Anyway, I see her staring at me.

"Psst, Eduardo?"

"Huh?"

The clerk repeats the price. "$228.50."

I guess that means I'm paying. "Highway fucking robbery is what this is," I mutter. I pull out my Visa card and hand it to the clerk. "No wonder I haven't been here for seventeen years."

"You get what you pay for," the weirdo with me sings.

"No, not really."

I take the tickets and put my hand on her back again, gently nudging her forward. The sooner we get in there, the sooner I can leave.

CHAPTER THREE

ED

We've been here for three fucking hours. Someone, kill me now. We did the tour of the entire place all while Bea rambled on and on and on about sea-creature trivia shit. Yeah, I know her name now. She seems to know everyone here, and several of them have called out to her by name. So, yeah, thanks to them, I was saved from that humiliation.

We did that penguin experience thing. It was okay. Penguins are kind of funny creatures. I know every fucking thing there is to know about them now. Just ask me. Go ahead. Ask.

So, now we're waiting in yet another line. This time for the dolphin show. Bea insisted we get in line thirty minutes before the doors even open so she can get her favorite seats before anyone can take them. So, we wait.

I look down at her. She's reading a handout about beluga whales. Apparently, they are now part of the dolphin show. "Here's something fascinating," she says with awe. "They can dive more than eight hundred meters."

"Mm-hmm." I mean, what else can I say? I know that's impressive, but I find myself not wanting to encourage her.

"And... oh my gosh! They can swim backward."

"Wow." Sorry, but there was nothing behind that "wow."

"You don't care, do you?" she says with her hands on her wide hips. "Can you swim backward?"

"Yeah. The backstroke."

"Not on their back, ass. *Backward.*"

Ass? I roll my eyes. "That's cool." I do my best to sound interested, but I'm past the point of giving a rat's ass—or in this case, a beluga's ass.

She harrumphs as she crumples up her brochure in her hand. Her face is turned away from me, but I can tell just from her posture that she's upset. "Look, uh...." What the hell is her name again?

"Bea," she mutters and rolls her eyes.

"Right, Bea, I've learned a lot. I'm just tired, that's all." And I want to get the fuck out of here and be by myself. Sundays are my day to relax at home and recharge. Now I have to recharge from this clusterfuck of a date—I mean outing.

"I was just trying to educate you about something that is important to me. Forgive me for assuming you wanted to learn something new."

"I do. It's just a lot for one day."

She turns back to me, her eyes shining. Did I make her cry? That's not what I meant to do. "You don't have to be rude to me. I was just sharing something I love with you. What do you love?"

Nothing. "Uh, sports?"

"Which sports?"

"All of them."

"All sports? All of them? Every team? From every land?"

"No." I chuckle. "Every land?" It's the first time I've felt like laughing all day. "I like the Cubs, Blackhawks, and the Bears."

"So, Chicago teams?"

"Basically, yeah."

"Well, we should go to a game sometime. I love hockey."

"You do?"

"Uh, yeah. Hockey guys are smokin' hot." She giggles.

"Right."

When the curtains open for the dolphin show, Bea takes my hand and pulls me quickly down the steps. "Hurry. We need to be in the front row."

"Okay." I've just resigned myself to this thing. I've got no fight left in me. Minutes after, we're seated, front row, center. The show opens with a short film about dolphins, their training, their habitat, and issues facing the mammals in the wild. In all, it is very informative. I'm surprised Bea isn't taking notes. She hasn't said a word since she plopped her ass onto the bench. I take notice when, as soon as the show starts, she slides her hand onto my thigh, giving me a gentle squeeze every time a dolphin or beluga whale does a stunt. Not gonna lie, her hand on my thigh is taking my mind right off of my bad mood. My thoughts are squarely on my dick right now.

I stare down at her small hand on me then over to her face. She's leaning forward in her seat, anticipating the next exciting jump or leap from the mammals. Her lips are shaped into a permanent "oh" as she watches, which makes my dick twitch. What is it about this crazy girl that gives me chills? And why, all of a sudden, do I feel compelled to kiss her breathless?

As my mind starts to picture her pink lips doing other nice things, I feel a sudden wash of cold on my face, chest, and lap. There goes my hard-on. "Fuck!" I shout.

"Shh." Bea giggles. "Kids," she says, pointing behind her. "Watch your language."

"We got fucking splashed." Drenched is more like it. I try to whisper, but I'm not very successful.

"We did. It's why I love to sit in this spot." She giggles again as drops of water fall from her eyelashes to her cheek and onto her shirt. My eyes travel downward. I can't help noticing that her white tee is practically transparent. I also can't help noticing that she's not wearing a bra. And the water was cold. Very cold.

Staring at her hard nipples, I hear her clear her throat. "Eyes up here, buddy." I jerk my head up and see her smirking. "Maybe, if you're a good boy, you'll get to see them."

"Huh? See what?"

She does this weird eye winking thing as she looks down at her chest then up at me. Then she repeats it. Oh, she means I may get to see her tiny tits. No thanks. I'm 100 percent a breast man. The bigger, the better. Hers are... well, they're small. Microscopic really. One of my hands could hold both of them with room to spare. But no matter. Her promise made me sort of speechless. "Oh." Oh? *That's all I can say?*

After the show, I tell her I need to get home. She's disappointed, but that's okay. I offer to drive her home, and she jumps at the chance. I don't blame her. The trek home on the bus would probably take her almost two hours. In my car, it takes just under forty minutes since traffic is next to nothing on Sunday evening. I pull up into her driveway and blink. Damn, she's got a beautiful place. I didn't see that coming. Her place has got to be almost a million bucks. "Nice place."

"Thanks. The land has been in my family forever. So, do you want to come over for dinner? Lasagna with homemade pasta, salad, the works?"

"Uh...." No. No way. *Say no, Ed.* That's a bad idea. A terrible idea. It'd only be encouraging her. I don't know what she wants with me, but I know I don't want squat from her.

"Well?" she says as she slowly lifts the center armrest from between us. She moves from sitting on her ass on her side of the car to crawling over to me on her knees. When she gets close,

CHAPTER 3

she slides her arms around my neck. "Eduardo? Please? It'll be my thank-you for taking me to Shedd."

Ah hell. I don't want to do this, but she's staring right into my eyes. It's then that I notice the color of hers. They're blue, but not really. Upon closer inspection, I'd say they are more teal with blue and green swirling around the iris. She scoots closer to me, and I feel that dang static shock again. When she reaches out and runs her hand through the top of my hair, I moan. Fucking moan.

"Does that feel good?" she says softly.

"Yeah." I used to love having my hair played with, but it's been a long time since anyone has done it. Years.

"Will you?"

"Will I what?" I say, distracted by the gentle sweep of her hand through my hair.

"Come to dinner, silly."

The part of me with sense knows I should turn her down flat, drive away, and never look back. The other part of me who's enjoying her hands on me is caving. Big time.

"When?"

"Tomorrow night?"

"What time?"

"What about six?"

"Sure. Yeah."

"Great!" She claps again and startles me right out of my fog. Then she wraps her arms around me, quickly gives me a kiss on the lips, and is out of my truck in seconds. "See you tomorrow." She blows a kiss to me, and I wave like a fucking jackass.

"Fuck," I grumble. "What was I thinking?" *I know you weren't thinking with your brain, Ed. That's for damn sure.*

CHAPTER FOUR

ED

At six o'clock the next night, I find myself in my truck with a bottle of red wine and a small bouquet of flowers, daisies, in the seat beside me. Why I decided to go is a mystery to me. I spent the entire day at work preoccupied by this dinner at Bea's place. I could kick myself for not saying no to this. I have absolutely no desire to date anyone right now. Or ever. Nothing good comes from dating or from romantic relationships. Nothing but pain and loss. I don't know where my pessimism comes from because I've seen the men and women in my life find partners, and they seem happy. Everyone but my dad. His partner, my mom, was ripped from him thanks to fucking cancer. So, there's a perfect example why relationships suck and why they're a terrible idea.

Don't get me wrong. I'm happy for Ethan and Ernie. They found their "one." But they're different guys than me. They sort of lead charmed lives. Dad and I took care of almost everything for them. They don't have any debt, thanks to Flynn construction, of which I'm now part owner. They've been spoiled and coddled their entire lives—most of it, anyway. The loss of our mom impacted them, but they were both too young to feel it like

I did. And I *did* feel it. I just wasn't allowed to show it. It would have upset Dad and my baby brothers too much if I'd let my emotions get the better of me. No, I had to stay strong and reliable. I needed to be the shoulder they could cry on and the man, albeit young, my dad could count on when he couldn't get out of bed after she died. I did what I had to do. I did what she asked me to do.

Just like I know what I need to do now. I need to cut Bea loose. It'd never work anyway. We're too different. She's my total and complete opposite. While she likes to talk, I'd prefer to sit alone and say nothing. While she seems to find joy in the life around her, I find joy in solitude. Also, in my work. I find peace and comfort in the quality of my workmanship in my home renovation projects. She's like a tornado spinning and swirling through life, and I'm... I'm not. I'm the calm before her storm. I'm the calm afterward. Calm. Stoic. Composed.

When I pull up to the curb in front of Bea's house, I put my truck in park and switch off the key. Leaning forward onto the steering wheel, I look to my right to peer at her house. It's fucking beautiful. This neighborhood, Albany Park, reminds me a lot of mine. There are pretty Chicago-style bungalows up and down tree-lined streets. From my vantage point, I can see a few of them need work. That's my cup of tea. It's how I got my house. It was in bad shape when I found it, so I bought it cheap when I was just starting law school and worked on it whenever I wasn't working for Dad or studying. The renovations on my place have been a labor of love, that's for sure.

I look back to Bea's place. It's a similar style as mine, Craftsman, but while mine is barely a story and a half brick bungalow with about eighteen hundred square feet, I'd say her house, with the same brick exterior, and two full levels are closer to three thousand square feet. Her driveway also has a brick portico off to the side, and if I lean back, I can see a huge, two-car garage with some sort of workshop or apartment above. I would never have guessed that Bea had money. She dresses like a vagabond. Damn, that's a nice place. I've got a garage, but it's a small one-car, so I had to choose whether I wanted it for my car or my tools. The tools won. I pull the key out of the ignition, sigh deeply, grab the wine and flowers, and hop down from my truck. "Might as well get this over with."

When the door chimes with the main song from *The Sound of Music*, one of my mom's favorites, I smile. It's loud and obnoxious if I'm honest, but it suits Bea. As the door opens, I hold out the flowers to get that part out of the way. "Oh my goodness," says a short woman in her fifties. "Those are lovely. You must be Eduardo." She says my name, or what Bea calls me, in a breathy, overly dramatic way.

"Uh, Ed. It's just Ed."

"Well, 'Just Ed,' come on in." She giggles. "My goodness. You're very tall, aren't you?"

I shrug. "I suppose." I'm not that tall, but I probably seem that way to her.

"How tall are you?"

"Six two."

"That's tall. Are you the tallest in your family?"

"No. My brother Ernie is taller. My dad is taller. But my youngest brother Ethan is shorter."

"Interesting. Okay, well, I'll get Beatrice for you."

Who the hell is this woman? What the hell is going on? Does she have a housekeeper or something?

The woman walks over to the bottom of a beautiful staircase that curves up to the left and disappears into an upper level. "Beeeaaattrriiccee," the woman calls, "Edddduuaarrddooo is here."

I hear "Okay" shouted from above, then the sound of pounding footsteps as she races down the steps. As soon as I get a glimpse of her feet at the top, I inexplicably hold my breath. She's barefoot, and as she descends, I see she's bare-legged too. I make a mental note that there is quite a lot of bare leg, but that stops on her thick upper thigh when I see it's covered by some sort of flowery, flowy shorts. As her torso appears, I see a matching top in the same flowery pattern. It's flowy as well but short. It seems light and airy. I catch a glimpse of bare skin at her belly. The entire thing is held in place by two tiny bows tied at her shoulders. It's a sexy outfit, which surprises me. I haven't seen her as sexy, really, until now.

When her face comes into view, I see her hair is piled on top of her head like the night of Ethan's wedding reception. It's messy but seems to be contained today. She has the same makeup-free face with freckles and full pink lips. Her eyes are sparkling and bright as she watches me look her over. "Well? Do I pass the Eduardo test?"

"Huh?" *The Eduardo test?*

"Do you approve of this outfit?"

"Uh, yeah." Why is she asking me that?

"Because I couldn't miss your sour face the minute you looked at my clothes yesterday. You turned your nose up at them."

"I did not." Yes, I did.

"You did." She leans over to me, and I get a whiff of something sweet. Her shampoo perhaps. Whispering conspiratorially, she adds, "Until my tee got all wet, then you seemed to like it just fine."

I feel the heat rise up to my throat. Embarrassment. I'm fucking twenty-nine years old, and I'm embarrassed. Jesus. "Yeah, well...."

"Did you meet my mom?" She doesn't let me finish my awkward reply. Thank fuck.

"Uh, your mom?" So, the housekeeper is the mom?

CHAPTER 4

"Mom, this is Eduardo. Eduardo, this is Genie with a 'G.'"

"Oh, right."

"You know, like *I dream of Genie?*"

"Right." I hold my hand out to her to shake, but she'll have none of that. She wraps her arms around my middle and squeezes. She pulls back and looks up at me. She's even shorter than her daughter, a bit rounder as well, but I can see where Bea got her body. Genie is pear-shaped as well. Her pear is just bigger than Bea's. Now I know what she'll look like when she gets older. Like I care. I don't.

"It's lovely to meet you too, honey." She turns to Bea. "Dinner will be ready soon."

"Okay. Thanks, Mom." Bea takes my hand, and I feel that weird, shocking sensation. This girl must produce static electricity by the barrel. "Come on, I want you to meet someone." She pulls me by the hand, leading me down a long hallway to the back of the house. Knocking on a solid mahogany door, she says, "Daddy?"

"Come in, sweetheart."

I watch as she pushes the door open, and I nearly choke from the shock of this room. It's like one you'd see in an old English castle. There are floor-to-ceiling bookcases around the entire perimeter of the room filled to the brim with books. The shelves look old, but I suspect they were added when this house was built. If I had to give an educated guess, I'd say that was in the 1940s. The shelves are stained in the same deep mahogany as the rest of the woodwork. I want to touch them, feel the grain of the wood, see how they're constructed, but my focus has shifted thanks to this odd girl pulling me further into the large space. And it is large. It's got to be twenty feet by twenty feet with twelve-foot ceilings.

"Daddy? This is Eduardo."

I look down and see a man about the same age as my pops,

mid-fifties, sitting behind a large desk that looks old and well built. There are stacks of papers strewn over the top of the desk, and a laptop computer is open on the side. The man has gray hair that's sprinkled with brown. His face is ruddy and worn, but there are laugh lines on the corners of each eye. His hair is receding at the top, leaving tufts of hair at both sides. When he stands, I can't help noticing how slight he is. If he's over five feet eight inches, I'd be shocked. "Mr. uh...." Oh, shit. I don't know her last name.

"Yousef. Jacob Yousef."

"Mr. Yousef."

"Call me Jacob, please, Eduardo."

"Please," for the love of God, "call me Ed."

"Not Eduardo?" he says, winking at his daughter.

"No, sir."

"Welcome to our home, Ed." He sits back down and picks up some papers from his desk. I guess he's done.

"Come on, I'll show you my room."

I look over at Jacob to see if he's going to object, but he never lifts his head from his paper. Yanking my hand again, she leads me out of the office, back down the hall, and up the long, winding staircase. When we reach the top, I'm not disappointed. The workmanship from downstairs extends up here as well. There are built-in cabinets in this upper hallway; several are glass fronted. I hesitate in front of one of those and see the tiny air bubbles in the glass. I can tell it was hand-blown, once upon a time.

"Come on, Eduardo. My room is right down here."

I follow her, but my eyes are on her house. When we cross the threshold to her room, I can't help noticing it's a stark difference from the rest of the house. First, the trim is all painted white. I cringe. I'm a firm believer you should never paint over this kind of quality wood trim. But this is Bea's room, so I suppose there are no rules in here. The walls are bright yellow, her furniture is white, and the floor is a lighter hardwood than the rest of the house. It's covered by several rugs of every color of the rainbow. There's a rug next to her bed that is covered in images of bees.

There's a painter's easel set up in front of the window and a small table next to it that holds her paints and other supplies. The painting sitting on the stand right now is abstract. It's all swirls of muted colors. There are thick lines and thin lines running throughout in black and gray. I stare at it and blink. It doesn't seem to fit the woman who lives in this room. It's too dark. Too gloomy. I turn to my left and see a large photograph of a cat hanging on the wall. It's got to be sixteen inches by twenty. The cat is yellow with deep gold and white stripes. He's wearing a bow tie and sitting on a velvet chair just his size. It's definitely a photo taken at a studio. Who the hell takes their cat to a photo studio?

"That's Mr. Barnabus Nibblesworth," she says with pride in her voice. "Isn't he regal?"

I'm going to answer my own question. Bea is the type of person to take her cat to a photo studio. "Who?"

"My cat. The one that, uh, passed on."

"He looks...." Oh, shit. What do I say now? He looks old, angry, and fat, but I can't say that. Instead, I go with "He looks like he was a good one." Okay, what the ever-loving fuck? A good one? I've never had a cat. Ernie claimed to be allergic, so we never had one. Not that I cared. A pet would have ended up being my responsibility, and I didn't have time for any more of those.

"Oh, he was," she says wistfully.

I move on from there and look at her bed. It looks like a queen-size mattress with a canopy above it in white. There's a quilt on the top with a yellow and black geometric design. I look around the room and see a trumpet leaning against the wall and an electronic keyboard. "You play?"

"Once upon a time."

I don't know what that means, and I don't want her to elaborate, so I keep looking around at all of her things. She's got one large bookcase that sits next to her piano. Like her father's, Bea's is filled with books, however one of the shelves is filled with knickknacks and doodads. I make a move to look more closely at the shelf, but I'm pulled away. For such a petite woman, she's pretty strong. I'm not a small man, and she's been able to maneuver me like a chess piece since the minute I walked in the door. This time, she pulls me over to her bed and presses my shoulders down until I get the hint to sit. Once I'm where she wants me, she slides between my legs and sits on my lap.

"So," she states with a sigh as she runs her fingers through my hair. I nearly purr.

"So?" I ask. This whole thing is surreal. Weird. Strange. "You live at home?" I ask, closing my eyes at the soothing sensation of her hands in my hair.

"I do."

"Why?"

"What do you mean?"

"Why aren't you out on your own by now. Aren't you in your late twenties?"

"Twenty-seven." She shrugs. "Lots of people my age still live at home."

"But why do you?"

"Because I love my folks. They're awesome."

"Okay. But don't you feel like you need your own space? Privacy?"

"Why?" she whispers. "I've got the entire second floor to myself. They never come up here."

When I open my eyes, I see her face getting close to mine.

CHAPTER 4

When her lips touch mine, I pull back and ask, "What're you doing?"

"Kissing you."

"Oh." She leans in, and I watch her, like in slow motion, as she moves in again. "Are you going to do it again?"

"Yes."

I turn my head toward her. I don't know why, but she's like a tractor beam pulling me into the sun. When her lips touch mine this time, I slide my arm around her waist. It seems much smaller than it looks. I open my mouth so I can feel her lips between mine. She sighs as she leans into me. When she wraps her arms around my neck, I pull her body around, so now she's standing between my legs. I know. You don't need to say a goddamn word. I'm an asshat. But she's all soft, and she smells so good, and it's been months since I've been with a woman. Sue me.

Bea presses herself into me, and I feel the hard peaks of her nipples against my chest. My dick hardens at the thought of them. I slide my right hand up and skim her left nipple as I kiss and bite her bottom lip. She squeaks when my fingers barely touch her. She's sensitive there. I pull back. "Was that okay?"

With a sigh, she responds, "Yeah. You wanna see them?"

See them? Is she talking about her breasts? "Sure." Like I said before, I'm a breast man. I prefer them big and full, but I'm also a man. If a woman offers to show them to me, who am I to say no?

She slowly unties the left bow on her shoulder then her right. It's sexy as fuck. When the second one is undone, the top literally slides down to her waist, revealing her tiny breasts. I stare. I stare some more. They're small but shaped beautifully, like droplets. Her nipples and the area around them are small, only about the size of a quarter. Plus, they're the same pretty pink as her lips, and they're puckered. I lick my lips.

"You should taste them. They're sweet," she says almost shyly.

I chuckle as I lean forward and swipe my tongue over her left nipple. "Jesus. They are sweet. Is that pineapple?"

She giggles in my arms, and it sounds like tinkling bells. "Yeah. The other one is cherry."

I turn to the right breast and swipe there. "Damn. How?"

"I rubbed them with lifesavers before you got here." She giggles again.

She rubbed them with candy? That's fucking awesome. I mumble my appreciation as I go in for more. I wrap both arms around her and pull her closer as I lean down and suckle her nearly whole. She moans and writhes in my arms, sliding her hands into my hair as she presses her breasts into my face. She's really responsive. I switch back over to the pineapple side and do the same. My dick is so goddamn hard it's somewhat embarrassing.

I'm about to slide my palm into the back of her shorts when there's a knock at the door. "Bea? Dinner's ready."

I thought she said her parents never came up here? *Shit.* That's all it takes. Three little words to make my dick lose all its mojo. Damn.

"Wow, Eduardo. You've got a very talented mouth," she says, pulling her top back up. She's having trouble tying the first strap, so I reach up to help.

"Here. Let me."

When she's dressed again, she grabs my hand. Before I can stand, she leans in and kisses me softly on the lips. "I can't wait to see what else you're good at, Eduardo."

I stand up, thinking *fuck yeah*, but that quickly turns to *fuck no, Ed. No.* Cut her loose. Doing my best to shield my feelings, I smile down at her and make my way to her door. The sooner I can get the fuck out of here, the better.

CHAPTER FIVE

ED

Dinner was delicious. Mrs. Yousef can cook like a pro. She made homemade lasagna, homemade garlic bread, salad, and homemade chocolate mousse pie. "Wow, Mrs. Yousef—"

"Genie."

"Sorry. Genie, that was the best meal I've had in months."

"Well, that's sad, Eduardo."

"Ed."

"You need to come over more often. Right, Bea?" She turns to look at her daughter who is smack dab in the middle of taking her last bite of pie. Bea wasn't shy about eating in front of me. She cleaned her plate and had seconds on the pie. I suppose that's nice that she doesn't feel the need to pretend she doesn't eat. I guess.

"Sure," she says, chewing. "Oops, sorry." She pulls her napkin up to wipe away some whipped cream that landed just below her full lips.

For some reason, I'm disappointed. I can picture myself licking that off for her, but I shake my head. "No."

"No, what?" asks Genie.

"No, uh, I haven't eaten this well in a long time. So, thank you." *Phew, quick save, Ed.* I set my napkin on the table and start to rise. "I'm sorry to eat and run, but—"

"You're leaving?" asks Bea, looking distressed.

"I have to work in the morning. Bright and early."

"Bea doesn't know what that is."

Okay, those were literally the only words her father spoke during the whole meal. Sure, he grunted a couple of times. He nodded. He pointed to the dish he wanted, but he said basically nothing up to this point. I guess I shouldn't criticize. I didn't say much either. It was hard when the two ladies at the table talked nonstop. I did learn a lot about her family though. For example, I know her parents are both teachers. I guess I should clarify, Mrs. Yousef *was* a teacher until she had Bea. Then she quit to stay home with her. Mr. Yousef still teaches somewhere. I don't know where or what subject he teaches. From the stacks of papers on his desk, I'll just assume it's English-related.

I also know he's from New York and he's Jewish. There was a pause in the conversation when Genie mentioned that. I just nodded and waited. I don't care if he's Jewish. What's it to me? She continued, telling me he moved to Chicago for a teaching job where the two of them met. Genie sighed after that part and looked over at her husband with glistening eyes. Yeah, I know. It sounds like I'm making this shit up, but I'm not. Trust me. They. Were. Glistening.

Genie's last name was Duncan before she married Jacob. She's of Irish descent, and her great-grandfather was D.F. Duncan of Duncan Yo-Yos. However, according to Bea, he was *not* the inventor of the Yo-Yo since it is the second oldest toy in history. Leave it to her to know that obscure trivia. I also know that Genie is not rich and that her parents blew the money that was left to them by her father. The house was left to Genie in her grandfather's will, so her parents weren't able to sell it.

"Thank goodness," said Genie. "The house will go to Bea when we're gone." Genie looks at me and winks.

Why did she wink at me? I have no idea. I'm brought back to the present when Bea giggles.

"Oh, Daddy. I've gotten up early before."

"High school," he mutters.

"Daddy, now you know that's not true," she defends. But the pink flush that rose to her cheeks tells me she's embarrassed about that.

"Oh, Jacob, don't be so hard on her. She's a free spirit." Genie turns to me. "I knew she would be. In the womb. She buzzed around inside my tummy the entire pregnancy. That's why I called her Beatrice."

I blink because I don't understand.

"You know? Bea. Like a worker bee?"

"Oh, right." I chuckle. "It fits, Mrs—" Genie glares at me. "I mean, Genie."

"It does," mumbles Jacob.

It does. I set my napkin down on the table and extend my hand to him. "Nice meeting you, Jacob."

"You too. Don't be a stranger."

"Oh, sure. Right."

I step away from the table and make my way to the door. I get halfway before Genie catches up to me and hugs me around the middle. "I'm so glad I got to meet Bea's young man."

Bea's young man? "Right," I mutter. In my head, I hear myself chanting *Run, Ed, Run.*

Bea steps up to the front door. "Let me walk you out," I say nothing as I watch her pull the door open. I wait and let her walk out first. She takes my hand the second I'm on her front porch. She pulls me out until I'm on the driver's side of my truck, hidden from her front door and, no doubt, prying eyes. "Thanks for coming tonight."

"You're welcome. Thanks for inviting me." I reach for the door handle, but she stops me before I can get it open.

"So?" she says nervously. It's not an emotion I've seen from her yet.

"So?"

She places her hands on either side of my waist. "When should we go out again?" Her nervousness is gone.

"Oh, I don't know. I'm pretty busy."

"What about Wednesday?"

"That's in two days."

"True."

"Can't. Started a big project this week. I'll be working late."

She taps her bare foot on the pavement. "Well, I can't on Saturday. There's a banquet I have to work."

"Right. Look, Bea—"

"Welp! Friday, it is. It's better anyway. Friday is date night. Do you want to go out or stay in?"

"Bea, I—"

"We could Netflix and chill," she says, raising her eyebrows up and down. "Or I could bring some DVDs. Text me your address."

"Bea—"

"What time do you think you'll get home on Friday?"

"Late. Seven or eight." There, that should dissuade her.

"That works for me. Here, hand me your phone."

I pull it out of my back pocket and hand it to her. What is it about her? I almost feel like I can't refuse her. She clicks around on my phone. "What's your address?"

"5042 West Deming Place." *Ed. Why? Why did you tell her your address? Now she'll probably be over all the time. Oh, fuck. What if she's a crazy stalker?*

"What neighborhood is that?"

"Cragin."

CHAPTER 5

"Oh." She clicks some more then looks up at me as she hands me back my phone. "I just sent myself your address." She leans up and kisses my mouth softly. "I'll see you Friday night."

She starts to walk away, but I stop her with my hand on her forearm. "Bea?"

"Yeah?"

The moon is bright tonight. It's shining right down onto her pretty face. A pretty face that is smiling up at me. I can't seem to say what I need to say right now. Cutting her loose in front of her parents' house seems cruel. I'll do it Friday night. So I just say, "Thanks again for dinner."

"You're welcome." Bea waves as she steps onto the curb. "Drive safe. See you Friday."

I hop into my truck and start it up. I wait until I'm down the block at the stop sign before I start banging my head against the steering wheel, literally. "Goddamn, I'm a pussy." I should have told her. Now I've got to worry about this shit for another four days. Fucking awesome.

CHAPTER SIX

ED

As I measure this kitchen in my current reno for new countertops, new everything, my phone buzzes in my pocket. My first instinct is to look at the caller ID, but when I'm at work, I just assume it's one of my crew, my dad, uncle, or a brother. "Ed." It's all I say when I'm at work. No need to be formal.

"Oh my God. Ed!" shrieks a woman.

I grumble at the voice. It's the same voice that called me around this same time yesterday. But I'm going to play dumb. "Who is this?"

"Bea. It's Bea. Oh my God, Ed. You have to come over here right now!"

Well, this is certainly different than yesterday's phone call. She only wanted to talk then, and Jesus did she ever talk. She talked about everything from sports to art. I remember it like it was yesterday. Ha, ha.

Oh, Eduardo. I've got so much to tell you. I read in the paper about a new exhibit at the Art Institute of Chicago. Have you ever been there? Well, if not, you have to go. I'll take you for sure.

This new exhibit is all about abstract expressionist artists from the 1960s. It's one of my favorite genres of art. The passion and color they used on their canvases is simply breathtaking. Oh, I also saw there's something new happening at Second City. I bet you've never been there either. It's a troupe of super-duper funny people who do improvisational stuff on stage. The last time I was there I got to go up and be a part of their scene. It was hilarious. I loved it. So, yeah. We should totally do that.

I said nothing for the five minutes she spoke since she didn't give me a chance to respond. It's okay. I think she just needs an ear, any ear. Returning to present day, I squeeze my eyes shut and concentrate on my breathing. I need to find my happy place. It's then I actually listen, and what I hear is unmistakable, she sounds scared. It could be excitement. I just don't know her well enough to be able to decipher her sounds, and I don't want to. I'm going to err on the side of caution and just ask. "What's wrong? Are you safe? Is someone trying to harm you?"

"No. None of that. You just have to come over here right now. I don't want to do this alone."

"Do what alone?"

"I can't explain over the phone. You just need to be here. Can you come? Now?"

"I'm working." Yeah, I can leave whenever. I'm the boss on this job.

"Please?" I hear her let out a sob.

Shit. "I can stop over in a bit. I've got to run errands anyway."

"Okay. Hurry!"

We hang up, and my first instinct is to pretend she didn't call. But the protector in me feels like there's something wrong—that maybe I need to go over there and make sure there isn't an intruder or something. "Fuck," I grumble.

CHAPTER 6

"What is it, boss?" One of my crew, Steve, asks.

"I gotta go out for a bit. Finish these measurements for me, would ya?"

"Sure thing, Ed." He pulls his own tape measure from his utility belt. "You comin' back?"

"Yeah. Be back after lunch."

"Cool. See ya."

"Yep." I unhook my belt and carry it to my truck with me. I've got some of my favorite tools in there, so it's not wise to just leave it sitting around. I hop in and start up my Ford F250. I bought this truck about a year ago, trading in my F150. This one has a king cab, so I can fit three other guys in here if needed. Plus, I've got an extended bed in back with protective coating sprayed on it, so I can haul lumber and other home-reno materials if required. It's a sweet ride. Bonus, I can write off the lease payments since I've got the Flynn Construction logo on the side. It's a win-win.

When I pull up to Bea's house, I see her sitting on her front porch on the swing. When she sees me, she jumps up and runs out to my truck. Today she's dressed down in a pair of cutoff denim shorts and a tank top with the picture of a glittering dolphin on the front. Of course, she's barefoot again, but she doesn't seem to notice the pebbles on the ground. She stops right in front of me and reaches up and wraps her arms around my neck.

"Oh, Ed. Thank goodness!" Pulling herself up, she kisses me quickly.

"Come on, come up to the porch."

I look down and see her ass, really, for the first time. Well, sure, I saw it clad in Wonder Woman panties, but it was also mostly covered by that short skirt. The other night, she was wearing loose shorts, but today? Today she's got on short, tight cutoffs, and hot damn, she's got a nice ass. Sure, it's wide, but it's also round and perky. I follow her up the steps, never taking my eyes off her butt. My dick twitches in my pants with every sway. Fuck. Calm down.

She stops right in front of the door. Pointing down at a large box, she asks, "Will you carry that inside for me?"

"Sure." I bend at the knees and wrap my arms around a relatively large box, about twenty-four inches square. Anticipating it'll be heavy, I'm surprised it feels only about twenty pounds or so.

She opens the door for me, holding it so I can step inside. I hear her mom from somewhere in the house and wonder what the hell's going on. "Can you set it down on the coffee table?"

"Okay."

She steps out of the room for a minute or two and returns with her mom in tow. When she gets to me, she looks up at me and blinks. "Ed, I can't open this. Would you open it?"

"What is it?"

"Just... just open it, please?" Her eyes are getting misty. Is she going to cry? Over a box?

I stand over the box and look down. Whatever the hell is in this box is scaring the shit out of her. It's taped shut with one piece of packing tape. I reach out and take hold of the end of the tape and tear it up and off the box. Bea gasps. I look over, and she's got her hands over her mouth.

"Are you sure about this?"

She only nods. I look over at her mom who is doing the exact same thing as Bea. What the hell is in this box? I pull one flap open then the other. I move the remaining flaps and peer down. It's something big encased in protective wrap. "Do you want me to take it out of here?"

Bea nods.

CHAPTER 6

I reach down and feel around until I can get hold of whatever the fuck this thing is. I hope it's not a fucking bomb. I'd hate to die this way. Lifting it out of the box, I can't help noticing how heavy the thing is and how oddly shaped. I look around for a place to set it when Bea pulls the cardboard box from the table. I set the object down on the coffee table in place of the box and stand up straight.

"Do you want me to unwrap it?"

"Yes, please." Bea sobs.

Jesus. I look around for the spot that connects the Bubble Wrap together. When I find it, I pull gingerly until it's released. I draw the plastic away and look down at the ugliest fucking thing I've ever seen. "What the f.... What is that?"

With a full-on sob, Bea drops to her knees in front of it. "It's Barney."

"Barney?"

"Mr. Barnabus Nibblesworth," says Genie as she comes up from behind me.

I blink down at it, and now I see it. It's the same color as the photo in her bedroom, but it's no longer in a cat shape. It's more, well, it's more abstract. "Um, did you have him taxidermied?"

"Y-Yes."

I know I shouldn't, but I've got to ask. "How? How did he die?" I think I can guess since it appears there's a leg attached where, I think, the tail should have gone. Whatever happened to this poor furry fucker wasn't pretty.

Genie replies, "Car. Hit by a car."

I almost choke while attempting to keep my laugh inside. I can't laugh. Both women are literally beside themselves.

"He looks so lifelike, Beatrice." That comment is from Genie. "Just like the day he died."

I nearly lose it again, but I save it by pretending I've got a cough. To cover myself, I ask, "What happened to his fur?" What fur? It's only got patches of hair here and there. "Did he lose it in the accident?"

"No," sighs Genie. "He had allergies. He licked his own fur off in patches. See there?" She points to his back end or what I assume is the back end. "He's got all his fur there because he was too big to reach it."

Oh, fuck. I've never wanted to laugh so hard in my entire life. I cover my mouth to hide it. My shoulders start shaking, and I can't control it. But Genie seems to misread my reaction because she pats me on the back. "I know, honey. It's hard to take, isn't it? Such a sad state of affairs for poor Mr. Nibblesworth."

Oh, shit. I need to step away. "Excuse me. May I use your bathroom?"

"Of course." She points down the hall near Jacob's office. I make it inside, shut the door, turn on the faucet and laugh my fucking ass off. Goddamn, it feels good. I don't remember the last time I laughed this hard. It's sort of cathartic.

After my fit of laughter subsides, I splash some water on my face that is now red. It really does look like I've been crying. I sort of hope that's what Bea thinks. If she knew I was laughing, it might hurt her feelings. Shit. Why do I care about that? It could've been my way out of this mess. Sighing, I open the door to the bathroom and step out into the hall. Approaching the front room, I hear the front door open and watch as Jacob steps up to the coffee table. He shakes his head and mutters only one word, that word being "Jesus." He turns and walks in my direction, no doubt heading to his office. As he passes me, he nods, "Ed." And that's it. No more words from Jacob.

I'd love to laugh again, but Bea is looking right at me. "Ed?"

I walk over to her and place my hand on her lower back. "You gonna be okay?"

"Yeah. Thanks for coming over. And for opening the box."

Why didn't she just wait for her dad to open it? And why is he home in the middle of the day? His school must be pretty flexible. He probably teaches high school. "You're welcome. I need to go, though. Gotta get back to work."

"What do you do?" She blinks up at me. "You know? For a living?"

"Oh, I guess we never talked about it. Construction. Home renovations mostly."

"Wow, that's neat. I figured it had something to do with that since you have that sign on your truck."

"Yep. Well, I need to go. See you later."

"So, where is your jobsite thingy?"

"Logan Square."

"Oh, I know that area. What street?"

"North Francisco," I say as I open the door.

"Okay, well, have a good day, darling." She giggles. "See you Friday."

"Friday?"

"Yeah," she says with hands on hips. "Date night? Remember?"

Shit. "Right." I turn to her mom. "Bye, Genie."

"Bye-bye, Eduardo."

I shut the door behind me and head back to the jobsite where I hope and pray I can think of something, anything, other than Beatrice Yousef. One thing I know for sure, I need to devise a plan to end this on my own turf Friday night. It'll be best for Bea.

THE NEXT DAY, I'm knee deep in the demolition portion of this job when I hear one of my guys yelling my name. I'm covered in plaster dust and other things I'd rather not talk about. These old houses can have all sorts of issues that can only be discovered once the walls are opened up. In this case, the problem with a sewer line caught me by surprise, literally. I'm sure I don't smell great.

"What?" I yell as I peel off a large piece of plaster.

"You've got company."

"Huh?" Who the hell is bothering me at work? "Tell them I'm busy."

"She says she needs to speak to you."

She? Who the hell? I set my sledgehammer down and back away from the mess I've just made. Stepping over debris, I stomp out of the master bedroom, down the hall, and out into the living room in time to see her. "Bea?"

"Oh, hi, sweetie," she says, giggling. "I brought you lunch." She holds up a wicker picnic basket in front of her. That's right, a fucking wicker picnic basket.

I put my hands on my hips, attempting to keep my temper at bay because I see my crew milling around us, no doubt trying to get some dirt on me. I don't need for them to see me lose it with this girl. It'll just add to the Flynn Construction fodder where gossip runs rampant and nothing is sacred. "Bea, this is no place for you to be. It's dangerous." Well, the room we're currently standing in hasn't been demolished yet, but the rest of the house has pretty much been gutted down to the studs.

She looks around and shrugs. Stepping closer to me, she says, "Looks fine to me; although, they really need to paint. This color is hideous."

"Bea," I say warningly. "How did you find me?"

"You told me what street and neighborhood you were working in; I just walked until I saw your truck."

"Kind of creepy."

She giggles again. Slapping my chest, she says, "Oh,

Eduardo. You're so silly. I'm just looking out for my man. I thought you might be hungry, and Mom made her famous meatloaf last night, so I brought you a meatloaf sandwich and a few other things."

My man? Ding, ding, ding, red flag. "Meatloaf?" Damn, I love meatloaf. That is if it doesn't have any weird shit in it.

"Yeah, it's really yummy. Do you have time to eat?"

I look at my phone for the time. "Yeah, I can eat."

"Good. Let's go outside. We can set this up in the back of your pickup. I brought a tablecloth, so we can have a picnic," she says, skipping out the door. You heard that right. She was fucking skipping.

Her skipping draws my attention to the dress she's wearing. It's sleeveless with tiny straps that tie at her shoulders. My dick twitches thinking about those little ties and what we did in her bedroom the other night. It makes me wonder if she's wearing a bra and if she rubbed anything sweet on herself for me. Oh, fuck. Now I've done it. I pull my tee down in front of me to hide the tent in my work pants. Shaking off thoughts of pretty pink nipples, I look at the rest of her dress. It's light blue with small flowers all over it. The skirt falls down to almost her knees, but as she skips, it flips up and down. I growl, knowing the guys are probably ogling her. I look down and see she's got on Converse again, this time they're the traditional off-white color. At least she's wearing comfortable footwear.

"Okay, if you'll lower that tailgate, I'll set everything up."

I reach out and pull down the back gate of my truck. There's dust and dirt all over the thing. I use my hand to sweep off the excess as she pulls out a checkered tablecloth from her basket. When I hear people chuckling behind me, I turn and glare at the assholes. "What are you assholes eating for lunch?"

The chuckles stop immediately. I turn back to Bea who is laying out a fucking feast. *That's right, fuckers, I'm getting a good goddamn lunch today*. There are several sandwiches, potato salad, coleslaw, potato chips, a small lettuce salad with two choices of dressing, a bottle of water, one can of soda, and a beer.

"Wow, that's quite a spread."

"Yeah, I probably went a tad overboard, but I wasn't sure what you liked. If you don't like meatloaf, there's a turkey sandwich too."

"I love meatloaf. I haven't had it in years."

I reach out and pick one up and bite. Moaning, I chew and smile. "Goddamn, your mom can cook."

"I know. She taught me how to do some things, but I can't do it like she can. Moms are like that."

I nod. I remember my mom's cooking. It was always perfect. I eat almost everything. I skipped the beer since I'm at work. I should feel bad that I didn't share my food with my crew, but those assholes were mocking me, so screw 'em. I wipe my face with a napkin she provided and rub my stomach. "That was good. Thanks."

"You're welcome. I'm glad you liked it."

We stare at each other for a second or two. She's looking shy right now. I see a blush creep up to her cheeks. I reach out and wipe some dust from her face. She blinks up at me, and I can't get over how pretty she is. It's too bad she's fucking insane. "You had some dirt there."

"Oh. Thanks." She moves in closer and steps up on her tiptoes. I lean down to meet her halfway. When her lips touch mine, I feel that electricity shit run down my spine. What the fuck is the deal with that? The kiss ends quickly when she only gives me a soft peck on the lips. Close to my mouth, she whispers, "Have a good day, Eduardo."

"Thanks. You too."

"See you for date night."

Oh, fuck. I forgot about that. "Right." I'm brought back to reality in a split second. I need to get out of that deal. This shit with her is getting too intense too soon. We've talked or seen each other every day this week. It's like she thinks we're in a relationship or some fucking bullshit. That isn't happening.

CHAPTER SEVEN

BEATRICE

I'm standing outside on Ed Flynn's front porch with my hand raised, ready to knock, but I stop myself. I need to get my nerves under control. Ed Flynn gives me all sorts of butterflies and jitters and other things that are much more fun. The minute I laid eyes on him at that wedding reception I knew. I knew like you know you've found the perfect dress because it highlights your best features and hides all the bad ones. I knew like I knew the day I met Mr. Barnabus Nibblesworth that he was someone special. I was at the animal shelter. I wasn't there to get a pet; I just liked going there sometimes to volunteer. That day, I went into one of the cat rooms that usually houses the "problem" cats. You have to have special permission to go into that room, and I had it. The head volunteer lady said they had a male cat in the room that was very close to getting *you know what*, because he was mean to everyone. He'd bite and claw at anyone who tried to pet him. When you have a cat like that in the shelter, it's usually toast for that animal because it means it would be too hard to place with a family.

Anyway, long story short—*too late**snort***—I plopped my bottom on the floor smack dab in the middle of that cat room and waited. I just sat. I didn't try to find a toy for him. I just sat and looked at my nails and daydreamed. After about twenty minutes in the room, I saw a yellow head poke out from inside one of those awesome cat tree houses. He looked at me, and I looked at him but then looked away. I stayed quiet and pretended like I had no idea there was anyone else in the room with me. It worked, because after another twenty or thirty minutes, he crept out of his hidey-hole and made his way over to me. I didn't try to pet him, but I did raise my hand so he could sniff me. After that, he went back to his hiding place.

I did that every day for two weeks until it got to the point he would come out the minute he heard my voice. The shelter named him Barney, so when I decided to adopt him, I added to that. He was a noble beast that deserved a name that fit him. He was big and long and very, very serious. There were times, though, that he would let me play with him. He always, always slept with me. He liked my mom and tolerated my dad, but he loved me, and I loved him. He was my best friend. Hands down. No matter how bad a day I had or how many people yelled at me and told me I was weird or strange, he was always my friend.

Taking a deep breath, I push my shoulders back and use all of the courage that Mr. Nibblesworth gave me, and I knock. When no one answers, I raise my hand again and knock. I wait a few beats but hear nothing. I know he's home. His truck is here. Maybe he's in the shower. Ooh, Ed Flynn in the shower. That's something fun to think about. I bet he's got a fantastic body. Heck, I can tell he does even in a snug tee and jeans—especially in a snug tee and jeans. The man is built. When I think I've waited long enough, I knock again. I lean on the door, hoping to hear something. Footsteps would be good. Even a television in the background would be a sign. "I know you're in there, Ed," I whisper to myself.

Geesh, I hope I didn't scare him off with my surprise picnic lunch yesterday. It was my mom's idea. She has always said that the way to a man's heart is through his stomach. Sure, she didn't think of that all on her own, but she says it often enough about my dad. He's always more cheerful after she feeds him. So, when she suggested I pack him up lunch and take it to him, I thought it was a great idea. Heck, she even made one for Dad and took it to the university for him.

I was so nervous walking up to his jobsite. That was only made worse when I saw Ed's face. I learned, quickly, that Ed can be cranky at times, but when I showed him the basket, he seemed to be amenable to the idea of a picnic and seemed to enjoy his lunch. He ate almost everything I made for him. I thoroughly enjoyed watching him eat. The man was hungry, like he'd skipped breakfast. I sat on the end of the pickup and nibbled on some grapes while he snarfed down my lunch. I smiled with pride when he patted his rock-hard abs and wiped his mouth off. It was a fantastic feeling that I'd done such a good thing for him.

"Okay, where are you, Ed?" When I still hear nothing, I ponder my options. I could: a) text him to tell him I'm standing on his porch, b) knock again, or c) which is not an option, I could leave. I opt for option b.

After knocking one more time, I finally hear him yell, "Just a second." I clutch the bag filled with DVD's to my chest and wait. And wait. What the heck? When the door finally opens, I smile, giving him my best one. But when I look through his screen door, my smile fades. "Did you forget I was coming over?"

"Uh, no."

"No?" If he didn't forget, why is he wearing the oldest pair of sweatpants known to exist in the Midwest and an equally old, ripped-up T-shirt that looks stained?

"No." He winces. "Maybe." He steps away from the doorway and walks further into his house.

Maybe? What am I supposed to do now? He didn't invite me in, not really. He didn't open the door for me. Do I leave, or do I walk into this house? I choose option two. I open the door and step inside.

"Shut the door. The air is on."

"Oh, sure." Something is off. He's acting rude. I caught that vibe from him the night of the wedding and a bit at Shedd, but I honestly thought that was just because he was tired and cranky. I'm not sure I can give him a pass on that again. I shut the door and walk into his main open-concept living room and kitchen. Okay. Confession. The only reason I know that is because I watch *House Hunters* on HGTV religiously. I know everyone wants granite countertops and stainless-steel appliances. They want walk-in closets and two sinks in their master bath. I shake my head at that. I mean, why? I don't get it. It means you have to clean two sinks instead of one, because seriously, ladies, do you really think your man is going to wipe the whiskers and toothpaste spit from his sink? Nada.

I stop daydreaming about *House Hunters* and take in more of his house. His walls are gray, and the trim is all stained light. I know that's also popular on that show. From my spot near the door, I see his kitchen is also gray, his counters look like white and gray marble, his cupboards are white, and his appliances are all stainless steel. Interesting. I see him bending in front of his fridge grabbing something. When he stands, I see he has a beer in his hand. One beer. He cracks open the bottle and takes a big swig. I guess I don't need a beer. I feel a burning sensation in my nose, the sure sign that I'm getting upset. I breathe in deep and smile. I'll give him the benefit of the doubt here and assume he had a crappy day. I step into the large living room and set my bag down. "So, what should we watch?"

He shrugs. "Not really in the mood to watch a movie."

"Well, what are you in the mood for?"

He raises one eyebrow at me then smirks. "Maybe a ball game. It's been a long week. I don't want to think, and this is sort of my decompressing time. I usually like to be alone."

"Well, you can be alone tomorrow night. You invited me—"

"No. You invited yourself."

"You didn't say no." Oh, shit. Here it comes. I feel tears gathering in my eyes. *No, Beatrice.* I'm not going to cry. He's just in a bad mood.

I hear him mumbling, and I make out the words "didn't get a chance," and I wince. This is not going well. He's turning out to be just as bad as everybody else. But I like Ed. I *really* like Ed, but this feels all wrong. "Do you want me to leave?" Because I will. "I'm sure there's a bus I can—"

"No." He sighs. "I don't want you to leave. You're already here."

Wow. That was encouraging—not. I hesitantly step into the kitchen. "Did you eat?"

"Yeah."

Okay. I guess it's late, almost eight. I should have eaten. He steps out from behind his counter and walks to his couch and drops down onto the seat, hard. When he doesn't offer to feed me or give me something to drink, I walk over to the living room and sit next to him. "So, what game is on?"

"Some baseball, but since the Cubs aren't doing as well as last year, that's not much fun."

"So, a movie?" I ask, encouragingly.

He rubs his face with his free hand. "What'd you bring?" He seems resigned to it.

I pick up my bag and set it on my lap. "Well, I picked six movies to choose from. I'll read them off, and you can tell me what you think. Sound good?"

"Sure," he says with an irritated sigh.

"One. *The Notebook.*"

"No! Next."

"Two. *Sixteen Candles*."

"Next.

"Three. *Miss Congeniality*."

That time he just stares at me. "Four. *The Princess Diaries*."

"Next."

"Seriously? You're vetoing *The Princess Diaries*?"

"Yep."

Sighing, I read the fifth movie. "*Rear Window*."

"Nah."

"*Hitchcock*? Grace Kelly? Jimmy Stewart? No?"

"No."

"Six. *Deadpool*."

I watch his brows arch. "Really?"

"Yeah."

"You really want to watch *Deadpool*?"

"Sure. I haven't seen it. I heard it was good."

"Okay." He takes it from me and walks over to his pretty state-of-the-art television and sound system.

"Your house is nice."

"Thanks."

"Did you buy it like this or fix it up yourself?"

"Fixed it myself."

Wow, getting him to talk is like pulling teeth. "You did a nice job... what I can see of it."

"Thanks."

So, he didn't take the hint. No tour for me. I slide off the lightweight cardigan I wore over to his place. It's still warm outside, but it matched my outfit so, yeah, I had to wear it. I wore one of my favorite dresses. It's pink and strapless with a sweetheart neckline. There are tiny navy stripes all over it, but they're so thin, it looks like texture rather than pattern. It's tight up top, and then it flairs out at my natural waist, so it does a

CHAPTER 7

good job hiding my hips and thighs. It hits me about midthigh so not too short. I've got on flip-flops with it because they're comfy. I knew I'd have to walk a good beat after I got off the bus, so I needed comfortable footwear. To top it off, I painted my toenails a bright pink color to match.

The thing is, I made an effort to look nice for him. I tried to blow-dry my hair, so it wasn't so curly (it didn't work), and I put on makeup. I shaved. Everywhere. Not to mention, I took a bus to his place. The least he could do is wear sweats that don't have holes in the knees. I take a deep breath. *No, Beatrice, it's fine. It's his house. He can wear whatever he wants. Perhaps he's never had a girl over.*

It's possible, although I highly doubt it. I mean... the man is good-looking with that thick, dark hair that's naturally messy-sexy. Even at the wedding, it was neatly combed on the sides, and then the top was long and sort of unruly. His hair is coal black, which looks fantastic with his blue eyes. They aren't your standard blue either. If I had to choose a tube of paint to match his eyes, I'd select ultramarine blue. That's a perfect match—not too dark and not too light. His lashes are dark and lush, which helps frame those beautiful blue eyes—eyes that show the feelings and emotions he tries to hide from everyone.

For example, I could tell he was sad that night at the reception. I can't tell you why he was sad, just that he was. At Shedd, he was annoyed. I can do that to people sometimes, annoy them. He was a sport, though, and hung out much longer than I thought he would. When he was at my house for dinner, I caught a glimpse of several emotions, including annoyed, turned on (yay me), curious, and confused. Yesterday, he was angry at first but happy after his belly was full of food. And tonight? He's annoyed again. Plus, he's got something on his mind. I know what you're thinking. You're thinking "How in the heck could you know that, Bea?" Well, I don't know how I know. I just do.

The thing is, Ed reminds me a lot of Barnabus. Both hesitant and wary of strangers. It took weeks to coax Barnabus Nibblesworth out of his bad mood, and I think it may take even longer with Ed. I don't know why Barnabus was so leery of strangers, and the same is true of Ed. I don't know why he is the way he is, and that's okay. I just know something happened at some point to make him like this, because his brothers aren't anything like this. They're social and happy. Ed Flynn is not.

As the movie starts, Ed settles back onto the couch, but he's moved to the other end. I don't like it. I cross my legs and arms and lean back into his comfy sofa and watch the movie. At about the halfway point in the movie, I stand. "Can I use your restroom?"

"Sure." He points toward the hallway that runs parallel to this room.

"Be right back."

I walk toward the room, keeping one eye on the movie. It's pretty good. Funny and kinda dirty. I had no idea what it was about. I just thought it was like one of those Marvel comic book movies, but it is and it isn't. When I'm out of range of the television, I race to find his bathroom. I open the door to an office space. It's dark, so I can't see much, but what I can see is nice and neat. The next door is another spare bedroom with a full-size bed and dresser. I push the next door open and voila! Bathroom. I slide my hand over the wall in search of a switch. When the light magically turns on, I gasp.

"Switch is out here," says a deep voice right behind me.

I can practically feel his breath on the back of my neck. A shiver runs down my spine. "Oh, thanks."

"No problem. Meet you back there."

In the bathroom, I do my business without snooping. I want to, badly, but I figure it's in poor taste. I wash my hands and wipe them off with toilet paper since I can't find a hand towel.

CHAPTER 7

Back in the main room, I see he's paused the movie. He's sitting on the couch in his spot, but he's waiting for me. "Um, do you care if I make some microwave popcorn?"

"I don't have any."

"I do." I walk over to my bag and reach down to the bottom below the other movies. Holding up the pouch, I make my way into his kitchen. I unwrap the bag, open the microwave, and start it up. It only takes three minutes. I ask him if he's got a bowl.

"Cupboard right above the microwave."

I open it up and see bowls of various sizes and also glasses. "Can I get a glass of water?"

"Sure."

"Would you like one?"

"Nah. You can grab me a beer, though."

"Sure," I grumble. I open his fridge and count 1-2-3-4-5 beers. You'd think he'd offer me one, but he doesn't. The guy doesn't seem to have any manners. When the popcorn is done, I pour it into a bowl, grab his beer and my water, and make my way to the couch. Before I sit in my original spot, I lean over and hand him his beer. Sitting down, I start to snack. "You can restart it now."

He clicks Start, then looks over at me, then at my bowl of popcorn.

"You want some?"

"Sure."

I take the opportunity to move closer to him. I scoot his way until we're almost sitting thigh to thigh. My dress has accidentally found its way up my thighs. As discretely as possible, I nudge it back down. When I look up, I see he's watching. "You look nice."

"Thanks." I wish I could say the same for him. "This movie is good."

"It is."

"Dirty."

"It is."

Ugh, I let out an annoyed sigh. This man is so frustrating.

"What's wrong?" he asks as he tosses some popcorn into his mouth.

"Nothing." I eat some popcorn, then sip my thirst-quenching water. A beer would sure be good right about now. We both turn to watch the movie just as another dirty scene begins. This time, they're doing it on the kitchen table, and she's got food all over her. It's hot—not to mention the fact that Ryan Reynolds is one beautiful man.

I wiggle in my seat as the scene progresses. It's turning me on, but I've got to remain calm. There's no way I'm making a move tonight. The minute that thought is out of my mind, I feel a warm palm on my thigh. Oh, hell. I look down at it as he gives my leg a gentle squeeze. I lean forward, setting the popcorn bowl on the coffee table. Without another word, I stand up and turn to face him. He looks up at me, and his beautiful, sexy eyes are hooded. I let my gaze slide down to his sweatpants, and I see they're tented. "This movie is hot."

He says nothing as he leans forward and wraps his hands around my waist. I'm lifted up and set down on his lap. With one hand behind my neck, he pulls me to him for a hot, wet, sexy kiss that's almost ravenous. I scoot toward him, so I can feel him between my legs. "Oh, wow, Eduardo."

"No, call me Ed."

"Ed, Ed, Ed," I mutter as he kisses me down my neck. I feel air over my nipples and realize he's pulled my top down to my stomach. As he latches onto my right nipple and suckles me, I arch into him.

"Damn, no fruit flavors tonight?"

"No. Sorry." I'm panting and writhing into him. His hard

dick is pressing into me in just the right spot. I reach down to feel him. I want to know how big he is without seeming like a giant slut. *Too late.**snort***. I skip the outside of his pants and slide right on in. "Commando?"

"Fuck yeah."

I push back and away from him.

"Where are you going?" he asks, panting.

I bend so I can nudge his sweats down. I want to see it. When I get them down far enough, his long, thick dick pops out. "Wow."

"You like it?"

"You've got a beautiful penis."

He chuckles.

"You do. But your penis looks angry."

"Probably because you just called him a penis. He doesn't like that."

"Oh, no? Does he prefer the moniker 'cock'?"

"Yes," he moans. "Definitely. Now wrap that hand of yours around him and squeeze."

"Bossy."

He grunts in response because I've done as he asks. I'm waiting for him to do things to me, but he seems to be content with my hand on him. I need love too. I stop my hand stroking and stand up. I reach beneath my skirt and wiggle out of my Star Wars panties. May the force be with me. I crawl back over him and smile. Nudging up further, I hold his cock out and place it at my entrance.

"Condom," he mutters through gritted teeth.

"No worries. I'm clean. You?"

"I'm clean."

I say, "I trust you," as I slide down onto him. "Oh, oh, Ed."

"Fuck, you're tight."

"Uh-huh." I press as far down as I can, then lift myself back up. His hands are now resting on the back of his sofa, his head back, eyes squeezed shut. I guess this is all up to me. I press back down and work up my speed until I feel like I'm about to explode. When I lift off like a rocket, he looks up at me and moans moments later. Then he stares. No words, just stares. I guess we just had a quickie.

I slide off him and bend over to pick up my panties as he pulls his sweats back up. "Gonna use the restroom." I practically run to the bathroom in search of a washcloth. I find one under the sink and proceed to wipe him from between my legs, muttering to myself all the while, "I'm such an idiot. I practically forced him to do it with me." Granted, he was turned on, but I'm the one who stood up and ripped off my own undies. What was he supposed to do? All he did was put his hand on my thigh, and I pounced on him like a cat in heat. I make a low, whimpering sound I know he can't hear. It's a sound that represents just how embarrassed I am. So very, very embarrassed. I use toilet paper to dry myself off and slip my panties back on. I need to get the heck out of here. I don't think I can even look him in the eye right now. He must think I'm a real floozy. "God, I'm such an idiot!"

Slowly opening the door to the bathroom, I peek out into the hallway. What do I think I'll find out there? A monster? I step out with my head held as high as I can muster. I walk out into the living room and see the movie has been paused, but Ed isn't on the couch. I look over to the kitchen and see him washing out my popcorn bowl. I look back over to the living room and see my bag sitting next to the table and my water glass on top.

I need a clean getaway right now. "Oh, hey, look at the time. I'd better get going," I say as I speed walk over to my bag. Picking it up, I turn and give him a fake smile. "Thanks, uh, yeah, for everything."

As I step toward the door, he asks, "What about the movie?"

"Keep it."

"You don't want to finish watching it?"

"Maybe some other time."

"Okay," he says, still standing in his kitchen. He's no longer washing the bowl. Now he's leaning on the counter holding a beer. "Talk to you later?"

"Sure. Call me." I look up at him as he nods. "Bye."

"Bye."

The minute I'm down his steps, I start to jog to the bus stop. I feel the burn of tears on the edges of my eyes, but I hold them in. I check the schedule and see the bus is due any minute. Thank goodness. I can wait to cry until I get home. I'll be able to talk to my mom and cry my eyes out. She'll comfort me and say all the right things. She always does.

CHAPTER EIGHT

ED

Fuck! What the hell is wrong with me? I did everything in my power to ruin tonight. I knew she was coming, but I intentionally dressed like a slob and didn't offer her anything to drink or eat. My mom would have been so disappointed in me. Hell, so would my dad. He's always a good host and a gentleman. I'm nothing but a rude, insensitive asshole. Oh, shit. I've turned into my brother Ernie.

I walk over to the table next to my front door and grab my keys. I can't let her take the damn bus home. That's taking "asshole" one step too far. I open the door and lock it behind me. Jogging to my truck, I hit the key fob and jump into the driver's seat. There are several bus stops around my neighborhood, so I head to the one closest. As I approach the stop, I see a female silhouette on a bench. Just as I'm about to turn to pull up to her, a bus arrives. I watch her stand and step onto it.

My shoulders slump, and I'm not sure why. Relief? No, I don't think that's it. Well, I'm relieved she's safely on the bus, but I'm not relieved she's gone. I hurt her tonight. I know I did. That beautiful light that she emits started to fade as the night progressed. She didn't deserve that from me. I'm supposed to be the fixer, the guy who makes things okay for everyone else. I did the opposite for her. Hell, letting her walk out into the night alone is so wrong it hurts in my chest. I let her down, but I guess I achieved my goal. I let her loose, and now I'm all alone. Again. Just like I wanted.

THE WEEKEND WAS UNEVENTFUL. Boring. I sat around and watched sports. My dad called to see if I wanted to get a beer, but I declined. Ethan called and invited me over to dinner so he and his new bride, Claire, could tell me all about their fantastic honeymoon. I declined. Ernie even called, although he didn't invite me over, thankfully. I was short with all of them, but they gave me a pass. They always give me a pass when I'm a moody prick. Granted, I'm not a moody prick all that often. Most of the time I'm pretty even-keeled. That's a skill I've honed over the years to make everyone feel at ease even when things were tense or unpredictable. I discovered the easiest way to get my brothers under control was being stoic and composed at all times. I've learned to keep all of my emotions in check, and it's served me well over the years. Except... except now I think being devoid of emotions is the problem. Beatrice makes me feel things that I don't want to feel. She makes me feel charged. When she sank down onto me, I thought I was going to fry from the electricity that ran through me. That's never happened before with a woman.

I'm not sure I deserve those feelings, but mostly, they scare the living shit out of me. She's not my type. She's my complete opposite in every way. She disarms me with one of her smiles and her stupid trivia. She's the last fucking thing I need—I do not need someone who makes me feel. I can't get attached to her because she won't stick, and I can't lose someone important to me *ever* again. Therefore, my best course of action is to just ignore her. When she calls, I'll let it go to voice mail. When she texts, I'll ignore it. I'm not going to block her; I'm not that kind of a prick. I'm sure it won't take long for her to get the hint. She's odd, but I don't get the sense she's dumb. She understands social cues, and being ghosted is one of those I can use to my advantage. It's unfortunate, but it has to be this way. It's for the best.

CHAPTER NINE

ED

What the hell? It's been two weeks, and she hasn't even sent me a text? What happened? What did I do? Yeah, yeah, I know. I told you all I was glad it was over, but I didn't expect her to be the one to end it. Was she that upset after leaving my place that she decided to never contact me again? I can't believe it. What kind of girl fucks a guy on his couch and doesn't call him afterward? Not the type of girl I thought Beatrice was. No, I thought she was the kind of girl who believed fucking a guy on his couch *meant* something. I guess not.

So, what now? Part of me knows I should just let sleeping dogs lie while the other part of me is pissed. There's even another part of me that's just a tad hurt by all of this. Getting blown off by the "weird girl" is taking a hit to my pride. I'm a fucking Flynn for fuck's sake.

My mind has been racing for days about this. Don't even get me started on the no-condom thing. I've never, in my fourteen years of having sex, gone without a glove on, but for some insane reason, I believed her. What if she's fucking pregnant? Jesus. *What have I done?*

I can't concentrate on my work. Thinking about this crap for the past two weeks has made me, how shall I say it? Unpleasant? Yeah, that's a good word for it. Thankfully, I have a crew who is always on autopilot, which gives me the luxury of being worthless. I've been pretending that paperwork is my number one priority while I hide out in my Flynn Construction office with my head facedown on my desk. Literally. Today is no exception. In that position, I moan into the pile of paperwork pressed to my face.

"Uh, Ed?"

Without looking, I know who the voice belongs to. Kennedy Corcoran, Ernie's future wife. "What?" I mutter.

"You sick or something?"

"No." Wait, maybe I am. "Yes."

"Which is it, dude?"

"Maybe?"

I lift my head up and see her standing with her hand on one hip. "One of your guys couldn't get ahold of you, so they called me. Inspector has some issues at your jobsite."

"Fuck. Great. That's just fucking great!" I yell at the ceiling.

"Whoa, Ed. What's going on?"

I sigh. There's no need to get Kennedy involved. "It's nothing. It's personal."

"Is this about a girl?"

I look away from her. "Maybe."

"Call Claire. She's wise beyond her years. Plus, she can keep a secret, which is more than I can say about your brothers. And don't trust me because I'll tell Ernie."

"Claire?"

"Yes, Claire. Got her number?"

"Yeah." Should I call Claire? Maybe. But I guess I need to actually get some work done. "I'll call her after I head back to my jobsite."

"Good plan."

CHAPTER 9

I watch her turn and march out of my office. Kennedy is nothing like I thought Ernie would end up with. I pictured him unhappily married to some blonde bimbo with no brains and huge rack, but he surprised me. Hell, I think he surprised himself. Kennedy is good people, and I'm happy for them both.

"CLAIRE?"

"Ed. Hey. What's up?"

I pause before I reply. What do I tell her? Do I tell her this over the phone, or do I ask her to have a beer with me? It is Friday night. Maybe she's got plans with Ethan.

"Hello?" she asks. "You there?"

"Yeah. Sorry. I feel like an idiot calling, but I need advice. Do you have time for a beer?"

"Sure, but it'll just be me. Ethan's at the theater tonight."

"Good. I know you can keep a secret."

"Ooh, I hate keeping secrets from Ethan. Is this about your dad and Penny?"

"No." What the hell is she talking about? Dad and Penny?

"Ernie and Kennedy?"

"No. It's about me. You can keep a secret if it's about me, right?"

I hear her mumbling to herself. "Sure. But I'm warning you, if it has something to do with Ethan, I can't promise you I can hide it from him."

"Deal. It's not. Meet me at Murphy's at six?" Friday night at Murphy's is going to be packed, but that's okay. There will be too much going on for people to pay any attention to us.

"Sure. See you there."

"SO, WHAT'S UP?"

Damn, Claire doesn't beat around the bush. We got our beer, ordered some wings, and she's ready to hear what I have to say. I clear my throat. "I met a girl."

Claire's eyes grow large and round. "You did? Where?"

"At your wedding."

"My wedding? Who? Was it one of my ex-work friends? Damn those bitches. No one said a freaking word."

"No, uh, she worked there."

"At the reception place?"

"Yeah, she was a waitress or whatever you want to call them."

"Banquet staff. She was part of the banquet staff?" Claire is talking excitedly. She's leaning over the table, so her face is now only about a foot from mine.

I shrug. "I guess."

"Which one was it? Was it that leggy brunette with the adorable pixie haircut?"

"No." Damn, where was she? "She has blondish hair."

Claire leans back in her chair and looks up into the air like she's trying to picture her. "Long or short?"

"Hair?"

"Yeah."

"Long, but it was up in a wild mess on top of her head."

"Did she have a butterfly barrette?" Claire's back to leaning forward, hands on the table. "The quirky girl?"

"I don't know. Maybe." Yep, she knows who it is.

"You've been dating the quirky girl?" she squeaks. "Oh, holy shit, that's fucking awesome, Ed. Her clothes were a hot mess, and she was super shy, but she was gorgeous." Her eyes get bigger. "Good for you, Ed. The girl was stunning."

Shy? "Yeah, well, things sort of went to shit real fast."

"What? Why?"

"Because...." I tell her about Shedd and dinner at her parents' place. I had her laughing her ass off about Mr. Barnabus Nibbles-whatever the fuck his name was, and then I told her about date night. I didn't tell her about sex on the couch, but I alluded to it. She got it without me having to confess. Thank God.

"So? What's the deal?"

"She hasn't called for two weeks. Not even a text."

"Seriously? She didn't text you back? When you tried to call her, did you leave a message?"

I look at her with a blank expression. "Well, I didn't call her."

"You sent a text, right?"

I know I look like a sheepish idiot right this second. "No."

Claire leans back in her chair and crosses her arms over her chest. Her happy just went down the shitter. "Seriously? Who taught you dating one-oh-one, Ernie?"

"No. I know how to date."

"No, you don't. Do you want to see her again? Because you're giving every indication that you were ghosting her." She doesn't let me answer. "Why would she have to call you? She made every single move up to that point, right?"

I nod.

"Shit, Ed. I don't blame her, honestly. I'd kick your gorgeous ass to the curb if you treated me like that."

I blink at her. I blink some more. "But...."

"But nothing. I think you have a decision to make, son."

"Son?"

"You prefer 'asshole'?"

"No." Jesus, when did she stop being sweet, shy Claire and start being this sassy person?

"As I was saying, you have a decision to make. Either you're in or you're out. If you're in, you're going to have to go all in. I mean, I don't know her, but I get the feeling she's a free spirit. Hell, she's probably out with a new guy right this minute."

"What?" I shout—too loudly. The table next to us turns to take notice.

"She's not going to wait for you to pull your head out of your ass, Ed. She's young and beautiful. Lots of guys dig a girl that's offbeat." She smirks. Claire's definitely offbeat with her video game designs and her penchant for blue hair.

"You think she's out with a guy right now?" I don't know why, but the thought of Bea with another guy makes me want to punch something.

"You could send her a text...."

"Right now?"

"Yes. Dumbass. Right now."

I'm not used to being the Flynn brother that's referred to as "dumbass" by Claire. That's Ernie. I sigh deeply and pull the phone from the side pocket of my cargo shorts. "What should I say?"

"What about 'Hello,'" she deadpans.

"Fine."

Me: Hi Bea.

"How long am I supposed to wait for a response before I send another one?"

"Longer than thirty seconds." She sips her drink, then smiles at the server who just delivered our hot wings. "Here." She points to the heaping pile of food. "Eat. It'll take your mind off the wait."

So, I eat. "Damn, this place has the best wings."

"Best everything," Claire says with her mouth full.

We eat in companionable silence all while I check my phone every thirty seconds. When did I become a teenage girl?

But, fuck, when my phone dings, I nearly spit out my swallow of beer. "It's her." I look down and read.

Bea: Who is this?

I hold it out for Claire to read, and she actually does spit out her beer. "Damn, she's a spitfire."
"You think she's fucking with me?"
"Uh, yeah. Try again. Send her another one."

Me: It's Ed.
Bea: Ed who?

Claire can't stop giggling.

Me: Eduardo? Ring any bells?
Bea: Oh, right. Eduardo.
Me: I'm glad you remembered. ;) What are you doing tonight?
Bea: Heading to work. Banquet.
Me: You work tonight? Does that mean you are off tomorrow night?
Bea: Yes.
Me: You want to get together?
Bea: No, thank you.
Me: No? What about Sunday?
Bea: No, thank you.
Me: We could go to Shedd.
Bea: That's nice but no thanks. At my stop. Gotta go.
Me: Okay. Have a good night.

I wait for a beat, but when she doesn't respond, I look up at Claire who looks worried. "Wow, she's done."

"Done?"
"With you."
"Done? With me? Why?"

She looks at me with a pitying expression. Shaking her head, she sips her beer. "Girl doesn't mess around. I give her props. I'm sorry for you, though."

"Hey, I'm not out of this yet. She's just pissed right now. I'll give her a couple of days and try again."

BUT I DIDN'T GIVE her a couple of days. I gave her about fifteen hours. At ten the following morning, I send her a text.

Me: How was work?

Sitting on my couch, I wait for her reply. It's Saturday morning, and I should be getting shit done—like my laundry, grocery shopping, and working out. My stomach is starting to look like Ernie's did when he was off work a couple months ago. I'm sitting in only my sweats, no shirt, so I look down at my abs and suck them in. "Definitely need a workout." Home renovation work is physical, but it doesn't really work the core all that much. I decide I can do things while I wait for her text. Keeping busy will be best, so I don't fixate on her—us. *Us?* Is there an us? If I had to go by the text exchange last night, I'd say no. But I'm not sure myself if I want there to be an "us." All I know is I don't like being the one getting blown off. Maybe this is all about my ego and nothing else. If that's the case, I should just end this. When my phone dings, I race from the kitchen and jump over the back of the sofa to get to my phone.

Bea: Busy.

Me: Tired?
Bea: No.
Me: What are you doing right now? Wanna get some breakfast?
Bea: No, thank you.
Me: Lunch?
Bea: No, thank you.

What the hell is the deal with "No, thank you"?

Me: I screwed up. Didn't I?
Bea: I don't know what you mean. Sorry. Gotta let you go.

There was some double meaning shit in the last part of that text. Yeah, I screwed the pooch on this one, as my dad would say. If only I knew what to do next. Maybe I should be doing nothing. I'm just so damn confused right now. One minute I want her, the next I think it's for the best that this thing fizzled out. I'm no good for her. I'd just disappoint her.

CHAPTER TEN

BEA

Dang it. I wish he'd stop texting me. Every time he does, I feel compelled to give in to him, but I can't. He's so gorgeous and complicated, two of my favorite things. All it takes is me remembering that night on his couch. When I do, I wince in embarrassment. I figured he felt the same since he didn't bother calling me for two weeks. One of the last things I said to him was "call me." When someone says that, it usually means "hey, call me," and the ball's in the other person's court. It did in this case, anyway.

When I got home that night, I went straight to my mom and dad's room. They were both still up reading in bed. I knew they would be. It's their thing. One of them, anyway. Another thing of theirs is getting up at the ass-crack of dawn to drink coffee together at the table in our kitchen so they can talk. This is going to sound like complete bull crap, but it's my dad that talks. Mom listens. It's sweet, really. I've heard their chatter from time to time when I've gotten up to pee or get a glass of water. Otherwise, it's their time.

Anyhoo, back to the night of couch-gate. I went to my parents' room and knocked on the door. It's not like I thought I'd catch them, you know, doing the nasty. **shiver** I did it out of courtesy. I heard Dad first. "Enter."

When I opened their door, Mom took one look at my face and jumped out of bed. She grabbed my hand as she passed me and pulled me into the kitchen. I guess she saw my red, puffy eyes. "Honey, I'll make tea. Start talking. I'm listening."

So, I told her. Everything. I know that sounds kinda weird that I told her about couch-gate, but it was a crucial element in her understanding my frame of mind. Mom didn't disappoint. "Now, honey, I'm not gonna lie and say I love that you had, um, relations on his Davenport." (For those of you who are younger than fifty, a "Davenport" is an old-timey name for a couch. Look it up if you don't believe me.) "But, I don't think you did anything wrong. You're an adult, and I know you think he's special."

"I did."

"I don't like that he wasn't a good host to you. He knew you were coming over, right?"

"Yes, but maybe he has a terrible memory."

"That's possible," Mom said, placing sleepy-time tea bags into our cups. "Maybe he had a bad day?"

"Possibly. It'd only been two days since we discussed it, Mom. He knew I was coming over. I think he was trying to turn me off; it was his way to push me away."

But I don't know that for sure. Honestly, I barely know the guy. I thought I knew him. The second he came to make sure I was okay at the reception, I felt a connection. When he spoke, I got goose bumps. His voice was so deep and rich. I shiver now just thinking about it. When I hugged him, it was like I was struck by lightning. Seriously, I felt like I'd been shocked. I thought it was a sign.

Ever since I can remember, I imagined I would know my person the minute I met him. I trusted in that knowledge. Sure,

CHAPTER 10

I dated some guys. I had to get some practice under my belt, so when I met *him*, I'd know what I was doing. Call it research. So, when I heard Ed, and I touched him, I knew; or I thought I knew, in that instance that Ed Flynn was my person. Apparently, I didn't know, though. Apparently, the joke was on me. Because, way back when I dreamt about meeting "the one," he felt the same about me. We'd both know it right that instant, and bam, that'd be it. We'd get married, buy a house, and have some kids, even though some of that list is impossible now. No matter. I never gave up hope for two out of the three. Until now. Now, I'm pretty sure my idea of meeting like that is complete and utter Cinderella bullshit. Leave it to Disney to screw with my head. Hell, I can't blame Disney. Wait, sure I can. If it makes me feel better, sure I can. So here goes: "Walt Disney, you're a rat bastard." Ah, so much better.

Well, not really all that much better. Three weeks after meeting Ed, I feel like there's no point meeting anyone now. I need to accept my spinsterhood. Embrace it. Once I'm done mourning Mr. Nibblesworth, I will go to the animal shelter and see if there's another big, yellow boy that needs a friend, because goodness knows *I* could use one right about now.

CHAPTER ELEVEN

ED

It's been another week without seeing her. I surprised myself and kept sending her text messages throughout last week. Some she's responded to, some she hasn't. I asked her things like how her day was, what her plans were, when she worked next, etc. It's fine. I didn't need her to reply, necessarily. I just wanted her to know I was still around, that I wasn't going anywhere. By the middle of week four, I resign myself to the fact that Beatrice Yousef is, in fact, done with me as Claire predicted. If I were a romantic, I'd just say "it wasn't meant to be," but I'm no romantic. I'm a pragmatist, so I'll embrace the fact that I probably dodged a bullet.

Things have gotten a little better. I've made a conscious effort to stop being the "surly asshole" my brothers kept calling me. I'm not completely my old self, but I've got my routine back like going to work and going home to my house to eat, then watching some television, and off to bed. There's nothing wrong with that. It's a perfectly nice life. I mean... I like my solitude, but I'm not a damn hermit. Take tonight, for example. I've got plans. I'm going out with my family—all of them. The entire Flynn gang, including wives, cousins, and their children. We're celebrating a contract for a new residential project. It's no ordinary project, though. This one is going to be a fifty-five thousand square foot home north of the city. Yeah, so a celebration is definitely in order.

My uncle Declan, my dad's twin brother, arranged for us to use a private room in one of his favorite Irish restaurants, The Galway Arms. Actually, his favorite place is Mrs. Murphy and Sons Irish Bistro, but they don't have a room large enough to house all of us. When I walk into the place, the first person I see is my brother Ernie at the bar. "Hey, Ern. Where is everyone?"

"Backroom. Still waiting on Hank, Sophie, Ethan, and Claire."

"Where's Kennedy?" Lately, I never see Ernie without Kennedy.

"She's back talking to Dad about something."

"Okay. I'll head back. Hey...."

"Yeah?"

"Get me a Jameson, rocks." I hear him grumble about money because he's a cheap ass, but I see him raise a hand to the bartender. "I'll pay you back, cheap ass." I'll need a drink to get me through this family crap. As I make my way to the back room, I see something in the corner of my eye, and I stop dead in my tracks, but I quickly recover. I don't want to make it obvious, so I keep walking. When I'm almost to the private room, I turn around and head back to the bar. I'll use the guise of getting my drink. I need to make sure I saw what I think I saw. And what I saw? Bea. On a date. On a date with someone else. From the bar, I should be able to see her table. If I'm careful, I'll be able to watch for a minute or two.

"Got your drink, brother. That'll be fifteen bucks, plus I tipped her five."

"Five?" I reach into my back pocket and pull out a twenty.

"What? She did a good job."

I look down at the one ice cube and half an inch of alcohol in my glass and wince. I'm a tad frugal as well. I'm switching to beer after this. I find a spot behind a large potted plant. There's just enough foliage to give me the cover I need. I peek through the large leaves and scan the room until I spot her. And him. Whoever the hell *he* is.

Since she's facing me, I take a good look at her. The first thing I notice is her hair. Most of it is down and wavy, but she's got parts that she's pulled up with some type of clip. How can her hair look so soft and shiny while also looking like a nest of varmints took up residence on top of her head? I can only see the top half of her, and what I see makes me both hard as a rock and pissed. The top half of her is covered, barely, with a yellow shirt that has her shoulders bare and seems to tie around the back of her neck. Does that mean her back is bare too? If so, that means she's not wearing a goddamn bra again. "Fuck," I grumble.

"Hey!" says a voice behind me. I'm so startled, I jerk and splash my million-dollar glass of amber liquid onto my shirt.

"Goddamn it, Claire. You scared the shit out of me." I wipe the excess fluid from my dress shirt and then onto my dark jeans.

Giggling, Claire covers her mouth. "I'm so sorry. I was just trying to say hello. What were you looking at back there behind the tree?"

"Nothing."

She moves around me and stands in my old spot. "Oh, it's the quirky girl. Is she on a date or something?"

"Apparently."

"You gonna go over and say hello?"

"No."

"Why not?"

"Because that'd be weird. She barely replies to text messages. She's not going to want me to interrupt her date."

Although, I'd love to get a look at the guy. I can only see the back of him. He's short, I can tell that from here. His head barely makes it above the table. Maybe he needs a booster seat. I snort.

"You're acting weird. Just go over there. And be nice. Don't punch her date or anything."

"Ha, ha. Very funny." Damn it, I'd love to punch her date. Sighing, I run my fingers through my hair. "Fine. I'll walk over there. But you stay back. I don't need any help."

"Oh, but I think you do, *mon frere*."

"*Mon frere?*"

"Yeah. It means 'my brother' in French."

I don't respond to that as I walk around her and make my way toward Bea's table. When I get there, I see Bea smiling and nodding. She's not talking, which is shocking; she's listening to the dude ramble. I slow my pace, so I can hear what he's saying.

"Yeah, I got this sick-ass plank, dude."

I watch Bea as she nods. Okay, I'm old, but I'm not dead. I know the fucker is talking about a skateboard. What a tool.

I step up to the table. "Hello, Bea."

Her date stops talking immediately, and I watch as she turns her head slowly to her left and up until our eyes meet. "Ed? What are you doing here?"

No Eduardo? Damn, that makes me sad. "Having dinner."

"Oh, yeah. With whom?"

Oh, is she wondering if I'm on a date? I wish I could say yes. Then maybe I wouldn't feel like such a fool right now. I look down at her. She looks beautiful. Her lips are pink and shiny, and her cheeks have a rosy tint to them, but I can still see her freckles. "I'm here with my family. We're in the back room. Celebrating."

"Oh." Beatrice smiles at me. Then she looks down at her date who doesn't seem very happy to see me. "Let me introduce you. Ed, this is Chet. Chet, Ed."

CHAPTER 11

I snort out a laugh when I hear his name. I'd bet you a million dollars his name is Chester, but the dude thinks it's way cooler for a skater boy to be called Chet. Jesus, the name matches the little prick sitting across from her. He's wearing a damn polo shirt, and it's pink. Not that there's anything wrong with that, but he's got the collar up like they did when my dad was young and a hoody over the top.

"You laughing at me, dude?"

Dude? How old is this guy? He can't be older than twenty-two. No way. "No. Well, yeah."

"Ed. Don't," says Bea warningly.

"I'm not. I'm just wondering why you're out with this guy?" I use my thumb to point down to the twerp.

"Ed."

"Bea," I deadpan. I'm waiting for an answer.

"Chet, will you excuse me? I need to powder my nose."

Chet looks at her like she just spoke French. He's too young to know what "powdering her nose" means. When she stands, I nearly swallow my tongue. Her fucking minimal, yellow top is attached to a dress that barely covers her ass. I follow the line of her legs down to yellow Converse. I step close to her as she walks so no one gets to see her scantily clad body.

"Ed, what are you doing?" she asks without turning back to look at me, which bothers me.

"Following you. We need to talk."

"No, we don't."

"Yeah, we do."

She stops in front of the ladies' room and looks up at me. "Look, we tried. It didn't work. You need to move on. Can't you see I have?"

"What? With that asshole?" I point back toward her table. "If he's over twenty-one, I'll eat my sock."

She stomps her foot down and slams her fists on her hips. My girl has some sass. *My girl?* Oh, fuck.

"So? What does age have to do with it?"

"You need a *man*."

She scoffs. Literally scoffs. "Oh, yeah? And you think you're a man?"

I lean in closer. "Oh, you know I'm a man."

She scoffs again, this time rolling her eyes. Slapping me on the chest, she turns and walks into the bathroom. It's okay. I'll wait. I don't have to wait long, when she steps out of the bathroom, she stops suddenly. "You're still here?"

"I'm still here."

"Whatever, Ed." She marches back to her table in time to see the shithead is no longer sitting at the table. Not only that, the dinner bill is on one of those black tray things. "Damn it!" she stomps again.

"Did the little prick ditch you?"

"Yes. And he stole my dessert."

I think she's more upset about her dessert than the guy. I pull my wallet out and reach for the check. "Here...."

"No. I've got it." She grabs it before I can. She pulls out cash, placing it with the bill on the tray. "All right. I'm leaving. See ya." She turns to go.

"Wait. Come to my family thing." Okay, what the hell am I doing?

"No. That's—"

"There's cake," I say with an arched brow.

"Cake?"

"And pie."

"Pie?"

How do I know there is cake and pie? Because it's a Flynn family party. Of course there's cake and pie. Sarah Flynn would never throw a family party without having tons of desserts on hand. And beer. Lots and lots of beer.

"Okay. For a minute." She starts to walk toward the back adding, "For the cake."

I take her by the hand and lead her to the room. She tries to pull away, but I clamp on just enough to keep her with me. "Ed, you don't need to do that. I'm fine. I'm just doing this because my cake was stolen." Without missing a beat, she adds, "Did you know the word 'cake' comes from Middle English kake, k-a-k-e, and is probably borrowed from Old Norse kaka spelled k-a-k-a. It is also related to the German word for Kuchen."

I smile down at her as she jabbers on about cake. If we ever play Trivial Pursuit, I want her on my team. When we reach the archway that leads to the party room, she suddenly stops walking. "Wow, there's a lot of people in there."

"Yeah, they were all at the wedding so...."

"Oh, right." She blinks but remains planted in her spot.

I tug her gently, and she finally walks with me. The minute we cross the threshold to the party room, I swear to God, every single Flynn stops whatever they were doing to look at us. It's dead silent. I think I hear crickets. That never happens at these family deals because the Flynns are a gregarious bunch. When my dad breaks the tension by yelling, "Dinner's ready," things go back to normal fast because the food is almost as important as beer to my family.

I feel her tense next to me. When I look down at her, I see her face is ghostly white. "What's wrong? Are you okay?"

"Holy shit, Eduardo," she murmurs. "How can one family have so much gorgeousness? It's not fair to us mere mortals. It's like Mr. and Mrs. Hemsworth had fifty more babies, only this batch was even better looking than their first one. Holy moly."

I'd laugh, except she's completely serious.

"You're good-looking too, Ed, but I'd say you fall into the

lower 25th percentile compared to the other Flynns in this room, which isn't bad when you see what you're up against."

I should be offended, but for some reason, I'm used to Bea's observations. "Yeah, so you've mentioned."

She looks up at me, and her white face is now pink from embarrassment. "Sorry. You're still very good-looking." She looks back out into the crowd, "Just not—"

"I get it." I chuckle. I actually chuckle. "I get it. Please stop. I don't think my ego can take much more."

"Oh, well." She blinks up at me. "If I were to compare you to the people in the restaurant"—she points backward—"you know, just you alone, I'd say you were definitely the best looking one out there, but in here...?"

She's interrupted when two of my cousins, Sandy and Emily, approach. "Hey, Ed. How's it going?" They're asking me but looking right at Bea.

I point to each cousin. "Bea, this is Sandy and Emily. This is my, uh, my friend, Bea."

"Your *friend*?" says Sandy in that tone that says she doesn't believe me.

"Yes. My friend."

"Well, Bea, it's nice to meet you. How did you two meet?"

I look down at her and wait for her to launch into some fantastical story, but she just looks back at me. Since when is she shy? "At Ethan's wedding. She worked there."

"You met that night?" asks Emily.

Bea nods. "Yes. Um, I was a server that night," she says, practically whispering.

"A terrible one," I scoff. I look down at her, expecting her to laugh with me, but she looks mortified.

"Jesus, asswipe. You ever wait tables? It's hard as hell. I did it through undergrad, and it sucked," defends Emily.

"Sorry," I mutter, looking at Bea.

CHAPTER 11

"So, you're a server at that banquet place?" asks Sandy.

I start to answer for her, but she finally speaks up. "Well, I do that sometimes. But, by day, I'm a mathematician."

I snort. "Bea, you don't have to be something you're not. We aren't judging you."

She looks at me and raises an eyebrow. She turns back to Sandy. "I do statistical analysis."

"Wow, you do that full time?"

"No, well, sort of. Just during the season."

"The season?" asks Emily.

"Yeah, the hockey season. I do stats for the Blackhawks."

I let out a ragged cough. She works for the fucking Blackhawks? "Why didn't you tell me you had a *real* job?"

"Well, first off, waitressing is a *real* job, and secondly, you didn't ask." She turns back to my cousins. "Could you please direct me to the cake?"

"Right over there." Sandy points to the far side of the room. "Here, I'll go with you. I need something sweet."

As Bea walks away, Emily pats my shoulder and mutters, "Well, cuz. I think you screwed the pooch on that one."

"I know," I growl. I'm always screwing the fucking pooch. A math-fucking-matician? She's right. I didn't ask. I didn't ask her anything. For all I know, she's won the Nobel fucking Peace Prize.

I watch as the girls walk over to the dessert table. I didn't steer Bea wrong. There are several cakes and a multitude of pies to choose from. I make my way over to my dad, leaving Emily and Sandy to take care of Bea. I find him sitting at a table with his brother, Declan, and his wife, my aunt, Sarah. "Hey, guys."

"Ed!" says my aunt Sarah as she jumps up from the table. Wrapping her arms around me, she whispers, "Are you going to introduce us to your girlfriend?"

"Sure. She's just a friend, though, Aunt Sarah."

"That's okay. I'd just like to say hello. She's lovely, Ed."

I search the room for her and see she's standing over in a corner with Em and Sandy. She's eating a large slice of German chocolate cake and nodding every once in a while as my cousins talk. I want to go over, but I think I'll wait. "I'll bring her over in a while. She's getting to know your daughters."

"Oh, that's good. She looks sort of terrified of all of us."

I look at her again, and I'd swear she's moved further back into the corner. "She's...." She's what? I don't know because I don't really know her. What I thought I knew about her was just tossed out the window the minute we walked into the place. "I'll go check on her." I walk away and head straight to her.

CHAPTER TWELVE

BEA

Standing in the back corner of this room filled with beautiful people, I feel awkward and ugly. That's not unusual; it's how I feel most days, but I wasn't kidding around with Ed when I told him he had a gorgeous family. I'm so self-conscious right now I'd like to move back further into the corner and somehow become absorbed into the wall, but no such luck; Ed is making his way over to me. I hope he doesn't make me talk to more people, because it's not my forte.

"How's it going over here, Bea?"

I'm still clutching my empty cake plate like my life depends on it. Anything I can use to pretend I'm doing something other than socializing is key to my survival in these settings. I know what you're thinking. You're wondering how I can wait tables at weddings and other events if I hate crowds. Easy. At that job, I'm working. I'm busy. I don't really have to talk to any of them. It's a job I don't really need, but I do it because I like keeping busy and it's good for me to be out amongst people. If I didn't do that job, I'd be sitting at home in my room reading e-books or painting.

"Good," I say as I look up at handsome Ed. "I think I'm going to take off, though."

"Why? You just got here."

I shrug. "I need to get home."

"Let me walk you out."

"Okay." I don't really want him to walk me out. I don't want him to convince me to give him another chance. That ship has sailed. Honestly, I'd like to just disappear without saying a word to anyone else. "Can we hurry?"

"Sure." He takes the plate from me and sets it on an empty table. Grabbing my hand, he pulls me out through the crowd and out the door. "Oh damn, I forgot. My aunt Sarah wants to meet you. Can we stop over there?"

"Another time?"

"It'll take thirty seconds. Believe me, I won't hear the end of it if I dodge her. She may be small, but she's a pit bull." He chuckles and smiles at me with his beautiful, straight white teeth, and I smile back. How can I not? When the man smiles, which has been rare so far, it melts me from the inside out. "Okay. Sure."

We walk side by side up to a table where several older family members are sitting. Even they're gorgeous. Sheesh. "Aunt Sarah?"

A tiny blonde woman stands up and steps behind a chair where a handsome older man is sitting. "Beatrice, is it?"

"Yes. Bea." I raise my hand to shake hers, but she wraps her arms around me.

"It's wonderful to meet you. I don't remember the last time Ed brought a friend to a family gathering. You must be very special."

I know what she's doing. My mom does it all the time. She's trying to get us to admit something, but I'm not falling for it. Instead of responding, I just nod.

"Bea? This is my dad, Donal Flynn."

I shake his hand then look to his right and see a pretty woman sitting next to him, but she's very young. Another sibling perhaps? She's too young to be Ed's mom.

"It's nice to meet you, Mr. Flynn."

"Donal, sweetie. Call me Donal." He turns, slightly, toward the woman on his right. "And this is Penny."

She's too far away for me to shake hands, so I give her a weak wave. "Hi."

"Hi, Beatrice."

I then turn to Donal's brother. At least I assume they're brothers since they look exactly alike.

"This is my uncle Declan," adds Ed.

I was right. I shake his hand. "It's nice to meet you." It's weird, though. Where's his mom? "Where's your mom?"

There's silence at the table, and then Donal speaks up. "My wife, Rachel, died when the boys were young. Cancer."

"Oh." I turn to Ed. I know I have pity on my face, but that's so sad. I slide my hand into Ed's and squeeze. Turning back to Donal, I say, "I'm so sorry for your loss."

"Thank you, Bea. It was a long time ago. Ed was eleven."

I nod and shiver, thinking about my mom—about what a car crash my life would be if she weren't around. She's my rock. My confidante. My best friend. I'd be lost without her. I look up at Ed and whisper, "I'm sorry."

"Nothing to be sorry about. It's life." The last two words are curt and short. It says everything I need to know. He's still hurting—all these years later.

We say our goodbyes, and Ed leads me through the sea of the magnificent Flynns, through the restaurant, and out the front door to the sidewalk in front of The Galway Arms. It's one of my mom's favorite haunts and one I'm very comfortable with, so I chose it for my date with Chet. Oh, yeah... Chet. I almost forgot about him. What a jerk! Why I let one of my banquet-serving coworkers talk me into a date with her little brother, I'll never know. I can hardly wait to tell her how he ditched me with the bill and stole my dessert. The bastard.

I pull my hand out of Ed's. "Okay. Thanks for the cake." I don't want to say "see you later" because I don't think that's a good idea—seeing him later, that is.

"Wait."

I turn around and see his handsome face. It looks sad. I step back over to him. "What?"

"I need to ask you something." He reaches out and takes my right hand into his. He tugs it until I'm close to him. I watch him lean down in slow motion, and I do nothing. When his lovely full lips touch mine, I lean into the kiss. What? Don't judge me. If you were standing next to one of the less-handsome Hemsworth boys and they wanted a kiss, you'd give them a damn kiss. I know you would.

He moves his lips over mine softly at first. His long fingers slide into my hair to pull me closer. I squeak when I feel his tongue slide into my mouth. When our tongues meet, I hear him moan and a shiver runs down my neck, over my nipples, and down to my belly. My goodness, the man can kiss. I move the arms that are just hanging at my side up until they're on his shoulders then around his neck. I pull myself up until my chest is touching his. My God, I want to climb him like a tree. When we hear someone from across the street yell, "Get a room," we pull away quickly. Whoa, that was some kiss. When I'm old and gray, I will probably remember that kiss. I will certainly remember the time I dated Ed Flynn, albeit briefly.

"I need to ask you something."

I nod.

"It's about that night at my house." He pauses. "On the couch."

I feel the blush from the kiss intensify on my face. "You have a question?"

"Yeah. You said you were clean. I told you I was clean. But we didn't use a condom. Is there any way you could be pregnant?"

"No."

"No? Are you sure?"

"Yes." Pretty sure. The possible percentage that I'm pregnant, statistically, is in the single digits. So, yes, I'm sure.

"Phew, that's a relief," he says, sweeping pretend sweat from his brow. "I'm nowhere near ready for a kid. Actually, I'm sure I'll never be ready."

"You don't want children?"

"No."

"But you've got such a huge family. You all get along so well."

"It's not in the cards for me. I practically raised my brothers. I'm done with that shit."

"Oh. Right. Because of your mom." I didn't need to ask. I know.

He steps back, taking on a defensive posture. "What the fuck are you talking about? This has nothing to do with her."

Whoa, hit a nerve there. "I, uh, I just meant you had to take care of them after your mom...." I can't say "died." I just can't.

"Oh, well, yeah. My dad was a mess. I needed to step in and be the man in the house."

"You were eleven?"

"Yeah."

"You had to grow up fast."

"So?"

"Did you get a chance to mourn her?"

"Jesus, Bea, of course." He walks further away. His face is

turning red, his expression almost hateful. "This is none of your fucking business, Bea."

That makes me flinch. He sounds so angry. "Right. Yes. You're absolutely right. I'm sorry." I turn and walk away, saying, "Take care, Ed." I move in the opposite direction I need to go, but I don't want to get near him.

"Bea?" I hear him yell from behind me. "Bea. Come on. Don't walk away. I'm sorry I said that."

I lift my arm and wave. "No biggie. We're good. See you."

"Bea? Let me give you a ride."

"No, thank you," I yell without turning back to look at him. If I look, I'll cave. So, I keep moving—faster now. As soon as I turn the next corner, I see a line of cabs. I open the back door of the one closest and slide inside.

"Miss, you'll need to take the cab first in line."

"No. I'm trying to get away from someone. Drive, please."

Sighing, the man pulls out into traffic as he picks up his phone to call someone. I probably got him into trouble, but I can't worry about that. When I look back, I see Ed standing on the corner, hands on his hips. I don't wave. I don't smile. And I know in my heart it's all for the best.

CHAPTER THIRTEEN

ED

Once again, I fucked up. I swear to all that's holy, she brings out the worst in me. I've never felt this conflicted about another woman before. Hell, I don't think I've thought about another person more than I've thought about her. What I don't get is why? What is it about this girl that makes me want to pull my hair out one minute and marry her the next? No, I didn't mean that last thing. I'm never getting married; I was just trying to make a point. Stopping at the bar on the way back to the party, I order another Jameson. A double.

"Ed, what happened to your girl?" asks Aunt Sarah the second I walk through to the party.

"Home. She went home."

"Why? This party's just getting started."

I shrug. "She was tired. And, truthfully, I was sort of an asshole to her."

"Too bad. She was a lovely girl. I liked her style. Quirky."

I smirk with the knowledge that Aunt Sarah is the second person to call her quirky. "She's definitely that."

My aunt steps closer and speaks softly. "I liked seeing you

with her. You were smiling. I can't remember the last time you smiled, Ed."

I nod as I sip my drink. "She's entertaining, that's for sure."

"No, it was more than that, and I think you know it. Why are you so scared to be in a relationship?"

I scoff. "I'm not scared. That's bullsh—" My aunt hates cussing, so I need to tone it down before she gets mad. "I mean, bull crap. Who said I was scared?"

"And defensive."

"Aunt Sarah," I say curtly, "I'm young. I don't need to be married with babies on the way just yet."

"Who said anything about all of that? You can be in love with someone without worrying about all that heavy stuff."

"Love? What the f—I mean, what the hell does love have to do with anything?"

"Ed, love has everything to do with it. That girl, Bea, was your perfect complement, except for her shyness. Otherwise, she's the yin to your yang."

"How would you know that? You talked to her for five minutes."

"Just a feeling. Besides, I know you, so I don't need to know her intimately to see something's there. You like the girl. You were happy to have her on your arm. I've never seen you like that."

"It's not what you think. She's crazy, Aunt Sarah."

"Crazy for you."

"She is not. She wouldn't talk to me for weeks. Hell, she was on a date with another guy earlier."

"Oh? Well, you've got your work cut out for you then."

I groan. "Aunt Sarah—"

"Now, you go make peace with your girl. You won't sleep well until you do."

I groan again, but this time it sounds more whiney. "Fine." I slam the perfectly good drink down on the table next to us. "But you're wrong about this, Aunt Sarah. You're way off base."

Chuckling, she pats my arm. "Believe what you wish, but I'm almost always right about things like this. But think what you want, honey. I love you, Ed."

"Love you too," I grumble as I leave the party. What did I let her talk me into?

AS I STARE at Jacob Yousef through his screen door, I see him standing in his robe and pajamas with his feet about shoulder width apart and his arms crossed in front of his chest. I can't help wondering if I've made a mistake coming here. I knocked, he opened, and then he stared. I asked if Bea was home, he nodded. I asked if I could speak with her, but he hasn't answered yet. "Jacob?"

"My daughter has come home crying twice in as many weeks. Each time after seeing you. I don't like how this is going. I'm afraid if there's a third time, I'm going to have to take matters into my own hands."

I snort out a laugh, thinking he's joking, but when I look down at his face, I see, very plainly, that he is not. He's pissed.

"Jacob."

"Mr. Yousef."

Hell, I've been demoted. "Mr. Yousef, it was a misunderstanding. I was rude to her, yes. That's why I came here—to apologize."

"Very well, you may enter." He turns and walks further into his living area.

I open the door and step into his foyer.

"She's upstairs." He turns to look at me. "But consider yourself warned, son."

I feel my shoulders slump from his reprimand. "Yes, sir." How did this short man make *me* feel three feet tall? I'm fucking twenty-nine years old; I should be over being scolded by my elders.

I jog up the stairs to put space between little Napoleon and me as fast as possible. When I get to her door, I hear music playing softly and voices. I can definitely hear Bea. Is she talking on the phone? Fuck, what if she's talking to that asshole, Chet, from earlier? Surely, she wouldn't give him the time of day? He stole her dessert.

I knock lightly on her door.

"Come in."

I slowly open it pushing my head through the opening first. She's lying on her bed, facing away from me. I can see her in her sleeping clothes, what there is of them. She's in a tiny tank top and even tinier shorts. Her arm is draped over something furry and yellow. Jesus, she's hugging that taxidermied cat. Is that who, or what, she was talking to?

"Bea?"

She rolls over quickly when she hears my voice. "Wha-what are you doing here?"

Her eyes are wet and puffy. I did that. God, I suck. I walk up to her bed and look down at her. I take the liberty of sitting on the bottom edge of her bed. "I came to apologize."

"You did?"

"I did. I lashed out at you, and that wasn't fair. I'm sorry."

She wipes her cheek with the back of her hand. "No, I'm sorry. I shouldn't have given you my opinion about something I know nothing about. I just wanted to help."

"I know." I place my hand on her bare knee. "I appreciate that, but my deal with my mom and dad is complicated. I'm not sure I even understand the depth of it. So, having you try to analyze me threw me off." I slide my hand up a bit then back down. "Your skin is so soft."

"Thanks. I moisturize daily."

I chuckle. "It feels like it." I wonder where else she moisturizes. *Okay, stop right there, pervert.* This poor girl is upset, and all I can think about are her soft parts. Ugh, I'm such a fucking tool. I want to lift my hand off her leg, but I'm not sure if I should. Sighing, she lays her head on her pillow. She seems to relax more with each soft swipe of my hand.

"You going to be okay?"

"Yeah," she says with her eyes closed. "Just keep doing that. It feels good. I like your hand on me."

Me too. "Okay." As I run my hand further up her thigh, I slide my body up so I can lie down behind her. "Scoot."

Bea scoots over to the middle of her bed, and I press in until we're essentially spooning. My chest is pressed up against her back, her ass nestled against my dick. Once we're settled, I move my hand up the side of her thigh and back down. "Is this okay?"

"Yeah," she says on a breath. "Don't stop."

Using my arm as leverage, I'm able to look down at the side of her pretty face. Her eyes are closed, and her lips are slightly parted. I lean down and kiss her neck, right below her ear. I feel need coursing through me. I continue running my hand over her leg, but what I want to do is slide my palm beneath that tank she's got on, so I can feel more of her body.

"Can I kiss you, Bea?"

Without responding, she turns her head just enough. I lean down and touch my lips to hers. Damn, her lips are so soft and sweet. Like candy. I swipe my tongue over her bottom lip, and she opens her mouth like she wants it as much as I do. Moving the hand from her thigh, I slide it up over her belly and breasts until I've got it wrapped gently around her neck. I move my head to the right, so I can get deeper into her. My dick hardens and thickens my pants in record time. Goddamn, I'm fucking desperate to be inside her.

When she suddenly pulls away, I know I've gone too far. "Bea, I'm sorry. I—"

"It's okay. You didn't do anything wrong. Can we just lay here together?"

"Sure." She rolls back to her original position, and I resume running my hand over her soft skin. I'm not sure how long we're like that, but I know it isn't long before I hear a sweet snore coming from Bea. The rhythmic sound is making me drowsy. Maybe I'll just sleep for a few minutes. I don't remember the last time I actually slept with a woman. I'm usually up and gone as soon as the sex is over. Since we didn't have sex, technically this is different. It's only sleeping. Nothing wrong with that.

Something wakes me from the best sleep I've had in years. A noise? When I feel something pressing on my dick, I remember. I slide my palm over a soft, round thigh that my whole body remembers, especially my dick. Bea is wriggling around, pressing that luscious ass of hers into me. "Bea?"

"Yeah?" she whispers.

"What're you doing?"

"Um... nothing?"

I chuckle. "It doesn't feel like nothing." I slide my hand over her hip and around her belly. Pulling her back against me, I press my hard-on into her. "See?"

"Oh, yes, I see," she whispers, then giggles.

"You feeling better then?"

"Much."

"You sure?" I ask as I slide my fingers just beneath the edge of that tiny top.

"Yeah, I'm sure."

Pushing my palm beneath the top, I move it up slowly. Her moan isn't loud, but it sure is sexy as fuck. My hand moves upward until I find one of her nipples. It's already hard and peaked. She presses her ass into me again, and it's my turn to moan. "Naughty girl, Bea."

"Mm-hm."

I rub my fingers over each nipple and then pinch the one closest to me. "Ed," she says in a breathy voice. Before I know what's happening, she's lifting her shirt up and over her head and tossing it behind her.

"You sure?"

"I'm sure, Ed. Only if you take off your clothes too."

As fast as lightning, I sit up and yank off my tee. I quickly stand so I can slip out of my cargoes and shoes. Standing in only my boxer briefs, I look down at Bea in just her sleep shorts. "Take off your shorts, Bea. Slowly."

"Bossy."

"Yeah, I'm bossy. Do it."

I watch as she runs her hands over her breasts, tweaking her nipples as she goes. My dick nearly jumps out of my boxers from that sight alone. Her hands progress down over her soft stomach and stop when she reaches the waistband of her shorts. "Now, Bea."

Giggling, she slides one hand into her shorts as the other one tugs at the side. I look at her angrily. She's making me nuts. *Now, damn it.* I think it but don't say it. She must be a mind reader because she uses both hands to slide the shorts down until I get my first glimpse of her pussy. It's nearly bare, with only a small strip of hair pointing down toward her beautiful pink pussy. I reach out and take hold of her shorts and drag them down her legs the rest of the way.

"Finally," I sigh. "You're fucking beautiful, Bea."

She blushes shyly, and that pink runs from her cheeks all the way down to her chest.

"Open your legs for me, Beatrice. Show me."

Slowly, she begins to open her legs. I rub my palm down over my boxers. I don't remember ever being this hard before. When she's fully open for me, I see her wetness. "Are you wet for me, sweetheart?" I swear I see her dripping after I call her sweetheart. "What do you want?"

"You," she whispers.

"Me?" I start to slide my boxers down slowly. "What do you want me to do to you?"

She's fidgeting on the bed as she watches me reveal myself to her. "Oh, God, Ed. Everything. I want you to do everything to me."

"Everything? Well, in that case, I'm going to start on those pretty little tits of yours."

The moan that erupts from her makes me leak all over myself. Fuck, she's sexy. Still standing above her, I lean down over her left nipple and lick, then move on to her right one. Damn, even without lifesavers, she's sweet. I move back to her left and gently suckle her into my mouth. Her body is now writhing on the bed. I lift my head, looking into her eyes that have gotten dark with desire. "What's wrong, baby?"

"Oh, Ed, I'm so achy, needy. Do something, please?" she whines.

"You begging me, Bea?"

"Yes, I'm begging you. Fuck me, something, please, please, please."

I move my mouth back over her nipple and suck, this time harder. I slide my left hand down over her stomach to her strip of hair. I glide my fingers over her once, twice, reveling in its softness. When she presses up into my hand, I push my palm down until I'm cupping most of her. She's so wet it's making my hand slip easily. Moving my thumb up, I feel her hard clit. When I find it, she practically screams.

"Shh, baby. Your parents are downstairs." Fuck, why did that statement make me think I'm still in high school.

"They can't hear. Their room is on the other side of the house."

"Awesome." I use my thumb and press it under the hood and start to circle her clit. As I do that, I slide two fingers into her, pumping in rhythm with my thumb. In minutes, Bea is going off like it's her first orgasm. "Feel better?"

"Yeah," she says coyly.

"You want my cock, babe?"

"Yes. I want your cock."

I slide onto the bed between her legs. They open wider, so I can find my place there. Her hands come up and slip into my hair. I moan at the feeling of her gentle fingers running over my scalp. I close my eyes at the welcome sensation. Her hands move from my head, down my shoulders, and over my chest, where she plays with my nipples. But when she slides her palm down my stomach and further, I nearly lose it. Thrusting in at that moment, I feel that electric shock again. It's so intense, I almost black out. "Fuck, you feel so good."

"You do too. Don't stop."

I won't. I pull back and latch on to one of her tits again. As I thrust back in hard, probably harder than I should, she squeals. "Harder. You can fuck me harder, Ed."

"You sure?"

"I'm sure."

I rear back once then thrust in so hard we nearly hit the headboard. Pulling out, I use my hands to urge her to roll over. "Hands on the headboard." She gets up on her knees and reaches out for her bed. I move up behind her, sliding my hands over her round ass and up to her waist. Up further, I bring them to her chest where I tug and pinch each nipple.

Placing myself where I need to be, I thrust up into her and get deeper than before. "Oh, God, Ed."

"Feel me, Bea? Feel my big cock?"

"Yeah, I feel you. Feels so good."

I press up into her and draw back out, getting closer and closer to my climax. I slide my palm down to find her clit again. Swirling my finger around and around, I feel her tense up and squeeze the ever-loving shit out of my dick. I nearly black out from the sensation. I come almost instantly, pouring myself into a woman for the second time in my life.

CHAPTER FOURTEEN

BEA

After the best sex of my life, I lie on my bed and watch as Ed Flynn stands up and picks up his boxers. He lifts first one leg, then the other until he can slide them up over his firm, round ass. Turning to look at me, he smirks. "Better?"

I nod because I'm not sure what he's asking. Sure, I'm better. Who wouldn't be after getting fucked by a gorgeous guy who knows what he's doing? But better? What is he really asking me? Do I feel better? Are we better? I'm confused. Even more perplexed, I watch him slide his cargoes back on then his tee. I didn't see him slip off his shoes, so it's no surprise I didn't see him put them back on.

"Welp," he says with his hands on his hips, "we good?"

"Good?"

"Yeah, are we good?"

"Yes." I still don't know what he's asking.

He steps closer to me, and I realize that I'm still completely naked and sprawled out on my bed like a damn floozy. I reach for my sheet and pull it up over me as he leans down. Thinking he's going to give me a passionate kiss, he surprises me, not in a good way, by kissing my forehead. "Sleep tight."

Sleep tight? That's it? No "Sleep tight, baby?" or what about "Sleep tight, sweetheart?" That's it?

He turns and walks to my door. Looking back, he winks, opens the door, and steps out into the hallway, shutting my door behind him.

Sitting up in bed, I stare at the door. "I don't effing believe this." He left. There was no additional cuddling, no plans made, nothing. It's like he thought if he fucked me, everything would be peachy keen, A-okay, hunky-dory, ducky. Well, it's not. I know I got up and ran out of his place after couch-gate, but that was different. Way different. This time, he was almost systematic in his methods to lull me into a false sense of a relationship. Hell, when you call someone "sweetheart" multiple times and "baby" even more, you tend to think there's more to this thing than "wham, bam, thank you, sir" sex. At least I do.

I lie back on my pillow and roll over to find Barnabus. He ended up on the floor beside my bed while Ed was here. "I'm sorry, buddy. I threw you over for another man. Well, rest assured, Mr. Nibblesworth. That will never, ever happen again. You're the only man for me."

CHAPTER FIFTEEN

ED

I check my phone for the hundredth time this week. "Why won't she write me back?"

"Who're you talking to?"

I look up to see my brother Ernie walk onto my jobsite. "What are you doing here?" Because I know I didn't invite him.

"Dad sent me over to watch you do electrical."

"Well, fuck. It'd be nice if someone told me I was going to have a huge fucking shadow today."

"Hardy har har. Asshole. He also told me you're acting like a prick to everyone and I'm supposed to cheer you up."

Now, that was funny. I throw my head back and laugh. "Okay, yeah, I needed that." If there's one thing I know about Ernie, it's that he's not the type to cheer anyone up. No, he's the type to piss you the hell off with his rude-ass comments and bad attitude. "So, how're you going to cheer me up?"

"With my wit and charm." He gives me a huge smile.

"You're in a good mood."

"Why wouldn't I be in a good mood. Hell, I'm in a great mood. I'm in love with the perfect woman, and I get it on the regular." He lowers his voice. "And I get it good, if you know what I mean. Because if you don't, I'll tell you, Kennedy Corcoran is the best fuck I've ever had."

"Okay, enough. I don't want to think about that the next time I see her."

Ernie's face gets dark and angry. "You fucking think of Kennedy like that, I'll beat you to a bloody pulp. She's *mine*." He growls the last part, and I'm not going to lie, it unnerves me.

"Jesus, Ern. I didn't mean it like that."

"Better not. Besides, I thought you were doing that curvy piece I saw at the party last week."

Me too. "Nah. John Donne had it wrong. I'm an island."

"What the fuck does that mean?"

Ernie's a computer genius—no joke, he's a real genius. He's just a little lost when it comes to real life and social cues. "Nothing. It means nothing."

"Okay, enough of this tea party talk. Tell me what we're doing today."

"We're waiting for the electrical subs to get here. You're going to watch them do the electrical."

"But I thought—"

"Nope. We're behind schedule. I had to get subcontractors in here for a few things so we can catch up on other shit. Electrical was one of them."

"Does Dad know?"

I look up at Ernie. "No. Why would he need to know? This is *my* job, *my* site, and *my* decisions."

He holds his hands up. "Fine. Sorry, bro."

"Sit tight. They should be here any minute. You can help them unload their shit."

"'That's not fair. What's your lazy ass doing?"

"When you are part owner of the company, you'll get to tell people what to do." I stomp off toward the master bedroom and bath, pretending I've got shit to do. I don't. All I want to do is check my messages one more time. "Why the fuck won't she reply to my texts?" It's been a damn week. I thought we were good. Fuck, I even asked. "We good?" She said we were. She nodded and said "yes." I heard her clearly. But I've been texting all week. I even tried to call twice. I didn't leave a voice mail because I knew I'd sound pathetic. My texts are bad enough. I scroll back to review them. The first one was that same night.

Me: Sleep tight, Bea.

She didn't respond. I got nothing. Nada. So, the next morning I sent her another one.

Me: I hope you slept well. I sure did. ;)

Yes, I used the winking emoji. Sue me. Then, at lunch, I tried again.

Me: I'm at lunch. I sure wish I had some of your meatloaf again.

Nothing like a double entendre to spice things up, if you know what I mean. Anyway, I didn't text again until the following evening.

Me: What are you doing tonight?

When she didn't reply again, I got the hint. It didn't mean I was just going to sit back and let her ignore me. Sure, I could go over to her folks' place, but I'm pretty sure they hate my guts. I'll risk their wrath if I absolutely have to, but not until then.

Me: Jesus, Bea. Answer me. What'd I do *THIS* time?

Yeah, I used shouty letters. When I got no reply after that one, I stopped sending texts. That hasn't prevented me from checking over and over again for a response from her. I mean, maybe she was in an accident and she couldn't get to her phone until today? What if she dropped her phone in a puddle and it's been drying out in a bowl of rice? Anything is possible, because it couldn't be that she's angry with me. It was good that night. Better than good. It was the best.

BY FRIDAY NIGHT, I've had enough. I need to find out if she got into some sort of accident or if she just hates me. Once I get that answered, I can move on with my life. I mean, seriously, I don't want to be in a relationship in the first place. I sure as hell don't want to get married and have a bunch of kids. I just thought Bea and I had something going that was fun. Maybe that's what she thought too, but she decided her fun was over when mine was just getting started.

So here I am again, standing on her parents' front porch like a pitiful fool. I waste no time. I knock and ring the doorbell. In no time, the door is wrenched open by Genie. "Ed? What are you doing here?"

"I'm here to see Bea." Why the fuck else would I be here?

"Oh, honey."

No. Either Bea is dead, or she's feeling sorry for me. Dare I say I hope it's the latter? I hate it when people pity me. I put my hand on my waist and wait. I know she'll tell me.

"She's gone."

Okay, that doesn't help. "Gone? She's dead?" It'd explain why she didn't respond to me all fucking week.

Chuckling, Genie says, "No, silly. She left."

"She left? Where'd she go?"

Genie turns her head, looking back to her living room. Next, she steps forward and speaks in a low whisper. "Las Vegas."

"Las Vegas? Why?"

"To meet someone."

"To meet someone?" I shout that loud enough for the neighbors to hear.

"Shh, we don't want Jacob to hear us, honey. He's pretty upset with you."

"I know. But Vegas?"

Genie nods. "I'm sorry, Ed. She and I both thought you were the one, but we were wrong."

She starts to shut the door on me. "What? What are you talking about?"

Genie changes course, pushing the screen door open as she steps out onto the porch. "Come on, let's talk by your big truck."

I follow her to my vehicle where she moves to the driver's side. She peeks at her house, probably making sure Jacob isn't coming out. "Look, sweetie, Bea is different."

I nod. I know this.

"Let me back up. Bea has never brought a boy home before."

"Okay."

"She always told me that if she ever brought a boy home, he'd be 'the one,'" she says, using air quotes. "When she met you that night at the banquet, she said 'she knew.'" More air quotes. "She said she felt a shock run through her the minute she touched you."

Shit, I felt that too. But this is all bullshit. "The one?"

"The one. Her person."

"Her person?"

"Yes. Her one true love."

I want to choke because this is Disney-sounding bullshit. "There's no such thing."

"Yes, there is, Eduardo. You're just not ready to see it."

"I'm very lucid, Genie. I like Bea. I like her a lot. But I wouldn't go so far as to say she's 'my person.'" My turn to use air quotes. "I don't want things to end with us. I guess I screwed up again because she didn't reply to any of my texts."

Genie nods. "Well, I don't know about all that. I just know she was ready to make a big change in her life. So, she left."

"Is she coming back?"

Genie shrugs. "I hope so. I'd miss her something fierce, but I've got to let my baby fly free if that's what she needs. Maybe you should do the same."

"Let her fly free?"

"Mm-hm, let her go."

No. Fucking. Way. "Which hotel is she staying in?"

"Ed. That's not a—"

"Please, Genie?" Okay, I sound fucking desperate. But if it works....

Sighing, Genie looks back at the house one more time. "Fine. It's the one that looks like Italy."

"The Venetian?"

Genie nods.

"When did she leave?"

"Yesterday."

"Who was she meeting? Is it a date or something?"

"Now, that's where I draw the line. If you want to go off half-cocked to Vegas, then do it. You can find out for yourself."

I lean down and kiss Genie on the cheek. "Thanks, Genie."

"You're welcome. But, Ed?"

I turn to her and wait.

"Don't hurt her again. She's a special young woman. She deserves happiness and someone who will give her that."

I nod because I don't know what to say to that. I'll think about that on my flight. Vegas, here I come.

CHAPTER SIXTEEN

BEA

I'm starting to think coming to Las Vegas was a bad idea. I knew I needed to get away from Chicago, from Ed, and all of my swirling, whirling feelings about him. I'm just unsure if this was the way to go. I didn't think about it. I reacted. A change was in order, so I sent my resume to the G.M. or general manager of the Vegas Golden Knights. As the newest NHL franchise, and I figured they could use someone like me. He replied to my email within the hour. His assistant set up my airfare and hotel accommodations by five o'clock the same day. That's all it took to get an interview for a brand-new job in a brand-new city.

So here I am in my hotel room getting ready for my dinner meeting with Kent Berones, one of the hockey operations people from the Golden Knights, to talk about my skill set and my work with the Blackhawks. Don't worry, I'd never give away any of their secrets. I love the Hawks. I don't want to quit working with them, but this may be the best way for me to move forward with my life.

Although I'm unsure about everything, I'm taking this seriously. Take my clothes, for example. I've decided to dress professionally for once. I pulled out the dress I dubbed my "funeral dress" for this meeting. Unfortunately, I didn't try it on before I left Chicago, because if I had, I'd have gone with something else. It's definitely tighter than I remember. When I first bought it a couple of years ago, it was loose and comfortable. Now it's tight—everywhere. Well, almost everywhere. Nothing is ever tight in my chest area, but the rest of it is very snug. It's got long sleeves and a scoop neck and is fitted all the way down to my knees. Holy moly, I've never worn anything this confining before. It's not that it looks bad, it doesn't. It's just my ass and hips are wide on a good day. In this dress, they're emphasized tenfold.

I peer at myself in the mirror at the dress again. It's plain and black, which is good. Black is slimming, right? When I saw how tight it was, I grabbed my one and only bra for an extra layer of protection just in case. I've even gone so far as to put on some makeup and flat iron my hair. It took me over an hour to get it straight, and since there's absolutely no humidity in Las Vegas, it should stay flat. Too bad it takes so long to get it this way. If it didn't, I'd do it more often in Chicago. I pulled it back into a sleek ponytail. I think it looks good with a simple dress like this one. It makes me look professional for once.

Checking my appearance in the mirror one last time, I shrug, grab my small clutch, slip on the black heels that go with the dress, and wobble out into the hallway. I'm not used to heels. Converse are my shoe of choice, but they don't go with this dress. At the elevator, I attempt to wiggle my toes around to get more comfortable, but it's useless. I step on and press the button for the main level. I'm supposed to meet Kent at a restaurant here in the hotel called Delmonico Steakhouse. They were kind enough to ask me if I had any food preferences, if I was a vegan, etc. I assured them that I liked everything.

At the restaurant entrance, my nerves hit me like a freight

train. I am terrible at things like this—meeting new people in new places. I clam up the minute I'm about to meet someone or the second I think I've got to converse with them. "Not tonight, Bea," I whisper to myself. I look into the restaurant, and it hits me that this place is super fancy. The restaurant is filled to the brim with tuxedo-clad men and women in glittering party dresses. I take in a huge lungful of air as I look down at my plain, black dress. Shit. I wore the wrong thing. In my head, I start the mantra that my mom taught me when I knew my nerves and anxiety was kicking in.

You can do this, Bea. Meeting new people and pursuing new experiences is an epic adventure, and I'm a brave adventurer. You can do this, Bea.

"Beatrice?"

I look up into the eyes of a gorgeous blond man. Well, *hello*, Vegas. Maybe this wasn't such a bad idea after all. Kent is tall—really tall, probably even taller than Ed. Oh crap, don't think about him. Luckily, this guy looks nothing like Ed. Well, except for that ruggedly handsome face and square-ish jaw. That's all. Everything else is different. For example, Kent's eyes appear to be brown, not blue, and Kent's nose looks like it's been broken a time or two. Ex-hockey player, I'd bet. All of those guys have bent noses. "Kent?"

He raises his massive hand out to me, and I place mine in his. Damn, no shock, not even a vibration. "Shall we?" he asks, extending his arm toward the restaurant.

"Sure."

Kent leads the way, and I notice he's wearing a suit that fits him perfectly. His butt is covered by his jacket, which is a shame because I bet his ass is nice. It's too bad I didn't feel a spark. He's probably married anyway.

We walk right in, bypassing the hostess, and make our way toward the back of the restaurant. Kent turns and asks, "Have you eaten here before?"

"No. It looks nice though."

He holds my chair out for me, and I slide into the seat. When he takes his seat, he says, "The steak is amazing. It's the only thing I've had here, but if you're not into that, I bet the rest of the menu is just as good."

I open the menu and salivate. I know I should probably order something light and small since I'll be talking, but I'm hungry. I haven't really eaten anything except snacks since before my flight yesterday. As I look at the choices on the menu, a waiter steps up and asks us for our drink orders. Kent orders a beer and water; I order a lemonade. Kent already has the job; he can drink his beer. "So, you work for the Blackhawks?"

Kent doesn't waste any time. He gets right to business, which is good. I can talk about work much easier than I can other things. I take in a deep breath and say, "Uh, yeah."

"You do statistical analysis for them?"

"Yes." I sit up taller in my seat. One of the only things I'm actually confident about is my math skills, or skeeeeels as I like to say.

"Billy Jones"—the Knights General Manager—"told me a bit about what you do, but can you explain it to me?"

"Sure. Well, I do more than just calculate general statistics. I do that too, but my work is really a combination of geometry, physics, and some calculus."

"Physics? Calculus?"

"Yes. I look at the way your team plays. I look at specific players and shots on goal, to find out which locations on the ice will earn you more points based on the velocity of the shot and the angle at which it's taken."

"But surely there are too many things that can go wrong. No play or game is the same. Each line that goes out onto the ice is different. Do you have to figure out everything everyone is doing?"

Before I can answer, our drinks are served. I sip my lemonade and look up. Kent sounds a bit confused about my job description. "I'm really only concerned with scoring."

Sipping his beer, he arches a brow. "I bet you are, you little minx."

Uh-oh. That was weird and gross. Red flag city. Ignoring his bizarre comment, I continue. "Um, well, I usually add a number of variables within my calculations. Did you ever hear of sabermetrics?"

Kent shakes his head.

"The movie *Moneyball* with Brad Pitt and Jonah Hill?"

"Oh, yeah, that was a good movie."

"It was. The real people that the movie was based upon worked with data using quantitative analysis. Theirs's was baseball, where they calculated everything about a player, including momentum and force when the bat hit the ball, etcetera. I'm just doing the same thing with hockey."

He chuckles. "You make it sound so simple."

"It's not simple, but it makes sense to me. My brain works like that."

Our conversation stops when the server asks for our dinner order. Kent orders a giant ribeye steak, country mashed potatoes, and buttered asparagus. As he orders, I quickly review the menu again. When it's my turn, I nervously point at something on the menu. When the waiter says it aloud, I wince. "Chilean sea bass?"

I look down at my finger, and sure enough, it's right on top of the sixty-dollar Chilean sea bass. "Well, let me see...." I look back up at the soup and salad section. "On second thought, can I please have the farmers market pears and lola rosa salad and the heirloom tomato soup?"

The waiter chuckles. "Those are great choices." I watch as he departs. My choices did sound good, and combined they only cost twenty-nine bucks.

"I've got to say, Beatrice, you seem too hot to be a nerd." Kent chuckles.

Wow, more weird words. Probably not the most appropriate thing to say in a dinner interview. It's helped me make up my mind about a few things, and as soon as dinner is over, I'll make my excuses and run back to my room. "Nerds come in all shapes and sizes, Kent."

"Apparently."

CHAPTER SEVENTEEN

ED

I didn't recognize her right away. When she stepped off the elevator, I had to do a double take because she wasn't wearing one of her typical crazy outfits. No, she was wearing a sexy black dress that was so tight I could see everything and heels. Where the fuck are her Converse? I'd bet she's got a black pair that would match. Not only that, her hair was sleek and shiny. Her ponytail ran almost all the way down to her ass. All I wanted to do was run my fingers through it.

Now, here I sit in the bar inside Delmonico's Steakhouse watching her eat dinner with a guy who looks like Thor. How the fuck did she meet this guy? Online? I wouldn't put it past Bea to go find someone online and fly off to meet him. It's so fucking irresponsible. I'm watching her closely as she talks and talks and talks to this man. Hell, maybe they're old friends—former lovers. How the hell would I know? I know practically nothing about her except she drives me fucking crazy. This guy could be an old boyfriend. Maybe someone from college? I have no idea.

So, yeah, here I sit like a complete dumbass in a bar, alone, watching her have a good time with someone else. I mean, it isn't like her last date with Chet. I knew that date was a bust when I overheard Chet jabbering on about skateboards. Besides, Chet was a boy; this blond dick looks like he's old enough to know what to do. Fuck. I hate this. I should turn around, walk outside, and jump into a taxi back to the airport. She's obviously made her choice, and I'm not it. I need to bow out gracefully. She deserves to be happy, just like her mom said.

But that's not what I do. Instead of doing what I think I should do, I torture myself by watching her through the entire dinner. When the waiter finally takes their plates, I'm surprised when she doesn't order dessert. She loves dessert. I watch as Bea stands up, wobbling on those fucking sexy shoes—shoes I'd like to see wrapped around my waist. I keep my eyes on her as she raises her hand to shake his. *She's shaking his hand?* Well, shit. No kiss? That's awesome! Oh, I mean, interesting.

She picks up her small purse thing and steps away from the table. His eyes are on her ass the entire time she's got her back to him. Goddamn, I'd love to punch that asshole in his fucking face. As she moves closer, I step back so she can't see me. I'm not ready to let her know I'm here, stalking her like a creep. No, not yet. I pay my tab and nearly shit when the bartender tells me I owe him thirty bucks for a glass of beer. I toss down a ten and a twenty and walk out. I see her off in the distance. She's meandering around the place, watching the gondoliers take guests down the fake Venetian canals that run through the hotel. This hotel is pretty cool, actually. I bet Bea has all sorts of interesting things to say about this place and how it compares to the real Venice. I wonder if she's been to Venice, or anywhere for that matter. I've always wanted to travel. When I was in high school, I fantasized about backpacking across Europe, staying in youth hostels, and living the life of a vagabond. But that's not the hand life dealt me. Not that I'm complaining. My life is good—perfect. I had a job to do, and that job was to take care of my family. So, I did that instead of wasting time and money doing dumb shit like going to Italy and France.

Bea is fascinating to watch as she checks out the faux buildings and shops that run on either side of the canal. I watch her step into a store that specializes in pastry. When she steps out, she's biting down into something that, even from where I'm hiding, looks delicious. Whatever it is, it's frosted with a white, creamy topping. Damn, I'm hungry. When she turns in my direction, heading back the way she came, I have to think fast. I jump into the closest store and hide behind a mannequin.

"May I help you, sir? Do you like that set? Is it for your wife? Girlfriend?" asks a gorgeous woman in a slinky red dress. I look down at my hand and see I've got my palm right smack-dab on the ass of the plastic person. A red-lace clad plastic person.

Thinking fast, I ask, "Do you have any superhero panties?"

"Superhero?"

"Yeah, like Star Wars? Anything nerdy?"

"Uh, no," she says, looking smug. "This is Agent Provocateur, sir."

"Oh, well, thanks anyway." I step back out onto the fake cobblestone street and search for Bea. I'm tall enough to look over most of the people, so when I spot her turning left into the casino, I jog in that direction, wondering if my girl is a gambler.

CHAPTER EIGHTEEN

BEA

The hair has been standing up on the back of my neck all night. It could be caused by any number of things, including the temperature they keep this casino. In a word, frigid. But this feels different. It feels like someone is following me, watching me. God, I hope it's not Kent. That dinner was so uncomfortable. He only said those two weird things, but he asked me too many personal questions throughout dinner. By the time he was finished with his steak, I wasn't sure if it was an interview or a date. He seemed put off when I excused myself after dinner. I thanked him and told him I'd see him tomorrow afternoon when I toured the Golden Knights facilities and met the general manager. The truth is, though, I hope I can avoid seeing him again. Awkward is the only way to describe the dinner.

Ignoring the nagging feeling of being watched, I look down at the ace and jack in front of me. I've got another winner if the dealer doesn't beat me. Blackjack is a fun game. I've never played it before, but since it's just a game of math, it's pretty easy for me. I watched some YouTube video tutorials on playing various games here in Vegas. I also read information on the

Venetian Hotel website and learned about the different tables and high-limit rooms. The one I'm currently sitting at has a twenty-five-dollar minimum bet up to five grand. I started with a twenty-five-dollar bet and have worked up to this two-hundred-dollar bet in a very short time. Since I keep winning, I feel like I should keep going. If I end up with nothing, I'll only have lost my initial bet. So far, I've been pretty successful considering I started at that amount and am now sitting with just over fifteen hundred dollars in front of me.

When the dealer busts, I watch as he places my chips in front of me. Yeah, I can totally see how people become addicted to gambling. I feel my blood pumping and my heart beating a million miles an hour with each hand. It's adrenaline pumping, for sure. Strange since I'm not much of a risk-taker in my real life. Vegas must bring out the gambler in me. I'd love to say I've got blackjack *skeeels*, but I'm pretty sure I'm just getting lucky.

CHAPTER NINETEEN

ED

"Holy shit," I whisper into the rim of my glass of whiskey. "She won again." From my spot behind a row of slot machines, I can see Bea perfectly. She's been playing blackjack for almost an hour, and I've watched her pile of chips grow higher and higher after each round. Several players have come and gone since she started. I can't help wondering if she's done this before—if she plays in her spare time. It's just another thing I don't know about her.

I watch as the dealer says something to her. She looks to her left then to her right at the empty seats on either side of her then back at the dealer. Shrugging, she sips her drink. Whatever she's drinking looks like lemonade. Since there seems to be a pause in play, I make my move. I stand up from my chair, walk over to the table, and sit in the seat to her right.

"Bea."

She looks over at me, and her eyes grow double in size. "Ed? What are you doing here?"

"I, uh, heard you were here."

"The hair on my neck and arms has been standing up all night. Have you been following me?"

"Well, yeah." Damn, she looks beautiful. Close up, she's even more stunning.

"Why?"

"Sir?" asks the dealer. "If you'd like to play, the minimum bet is twenty-five dollars."

I pull out my wallet and hand him a fifty. "Twenty-five, please." He gives me five five-dollar chips, which I place in my betting circle. I've only played blackjack a handful of times, but I should be able to remember the basics.

I watch as Bea sets down three one-hundred-dollar chips. "Three hundred?" I ask as the dealer places two cards in front of me.

She shrugs. "Seriously, what are you doing here, Ed? You shouldn't...." Bea stops talking when the dealer lays out our cards. I'm dealt an eight and a five. Bea gets an ace and a jack of spades—blackjack. When a waitress approaches, I order myself a Jameson and ask Bea for her drink. "Long Island lemonade, please," she says, smiling at the waitress.

"Your mom told me you were here."

"I'm going to strangle her," Bea grumbles.

"Don't. She saw how worried I was when I hadn't heard from you all week."

"Ed...."

I tap the table with two of my fingers to let the dealer know to hit me. I need another card to add to my eight and five. When he lays down a ten of hearts, I feel my shoulders slump. Twenty-three. Busted. I watch as Bea waves off the dealer since she's already got a blackjack. We both watch as the dealer has to stand at seventeen. Bea wins again. I watch as he places four hundred and fifty dollars in front of her. "Wow, you're really doing well at this game."

She shrugs. "Just luck."

Sure, there's luck involved, but Bea is a math whiz. I'm sure this comes easier for her than ordinary people. I watch her set out another bet, this time four hundred dollars. I stick with my twenty-five-dollar bet, asking the dealer for more chips. When we both win this time, I'm excited to see my twenty-five dollars grow by one and a half. I watch as the dealer counts out the six hundred she won. Beatrice stands up and pushes her chips to the dealer so he can replace her chips with larger denominations. I guess she's done playing.

"What're you doing, Bea?"

"Leaving."

"Why? You're winning."

She looks up at me and blinks. "Ed, why are you here?"

"I told you."

"You flew all the way to Vegas because, why? You missed me? You were worried about me?"

I watch the waitress set our drinks down just as Bea places her chips in her purse. "Yes."

Sighing, she picks up her purse and her drink, smiling and tipping the dealer before she leaves. "Thank you. That was fun." She turns back to me. "Come on, let's go somewhere more private."

I follow her through the sea of people, slot machines, and table games to a bar area that is open to everything. We get lucky and find a small table in the back. Bea sits first, taking the chair that faces all the action. I take the other. Sipping her drink, she looks at me. I sip my drink and take her in again.

"You look beautiful tonight."

She rolls her eyes. "Not surprising you'd like this look." She points at her dress. "This is my funeral dress. I only wear this for serious occasions."

"A date with Thor? Is that a serious occasion?"

Bea's eyes grow double in size again. "You were watching me at dinner?"

"Yeah."

"Ed, that's—"

"Creepy. Yeah, I know. Sorry."

Bea takes several gulps of her drink after my admission. Setting her glass down, she leans forward. "Look, Ed, this isn't going to work between us."

I lean in to her. I'm ready for battle. "Why not?"

Bea scoots her seat closer to me. "Because the last time we were, um, together, you got up, got dressed, and left."

"So?"

"So? You didn't even hug me afterward, Ed. You just left."

It's my turn to blink. "You wanted me to stay?"

She doesn't answer; she only nods.

"Bea, we were at your parents' house. I'm pretty sure your dad hates me. I didn't want to wake up with him standing over your bed with a shotgun in his hand."

Bea giggles. "My dad doesn't own a gun." She shrugs. "At least not that I know of."

"Funny." I sip the last of my whiskey. "If you'd wanted me to stay, you should have told me."

"You didn't seem like you wanted to stay. Quite the opposite, actually. I felt like you couldn't wait to get as far away from me as possible."

"I sent you a text that night. And the next day. And the day after that and the day after that."

"I know." Her shoulders slump as she drinks the last of her cocktail.

"Want another?" I ask, pointing to her glass.

"Sure, why not?"

I step up to the bar for our order and look back at her. She's looking out into the casino and biting her bottom lip. I turn to deal with the check and our drinks, but when I turn back, a man is sitting in my seat, talking to Bea. He's about my age, maybe a little older. He's leaning toward my girl saying something. She's nodding. She's fucking smiling. I take a second to look at the asshole. His dark hair is slicked back with product. He's dressed in a black suit with a black shirt and black tie. He looks like he belongs in a mafia movie. I step up to the table and look down at him. "You're in my seat."

"Oh, pardon me," he says in a Jersey accent. No joke. "I couldn't help myself. I saw this beautiful creature sitting here all alone."

"She's not alone. She's with me." The guy stands, and I'm still looking down at him. Short. "Thanks, but I've got this covered." I nod toward Bea, leaning down to say, "She's mine."

"Yours? You sure about that?"

I look at Bea's hands. They're winding around each other nervously. "Yeah, I'm sure."

Mafia guy turns back to Bea. He reaches into his pocket and pulls out a black business card. "If you change your mind, call me."

Fucking asshole. I'd love to tear the fucking card right out of her hand, right in front of him, but I don't get the chance. She places it in her purse. "Thank you, Tony."

"Tony?" I look at the guy. So fucking cliché.

"Mr. Russo to you." He turns on his shiny black shoes and leaves.

As I place her drink in front of her, she looks up at me with a rare, angry expression. "What? You're mad at *me*? The guy was poaching."

"Poaching?"

"Yeah. Poaching. He was hitting on my girl."

"Your girl?"

"Yeah, Bea. *My girl*. You're my girl."

"So, does that make you mine too?"

"Of course."

"Are you drunk?"

"No." Okay, maybe slightly. I've had a couple of beers, and this is my third whiskey.

She takes a big gulp of her drink then stands. "Well, boyfriend, let's go gamble."

Boyfriend? I like the sound of that. "Sounds good to me, but first, I need a kiss from my girlfriend. I haven't seen you for a week."

"Not here."

I'd love to kiss her here since Tony's watching us from the other side of the room. *Fucker.* Instead, I take her by the hand and lead her out of the bustling bar into the casino. I move to the outer edge of the enormous room, looking for somewhere private. When I find a secluded spot between two slot machines, I take her drink from her and set it down next to mine. "Now?"

She nods. I reach out to her waist, sliding my hands around her back. Pulling her into me, I lean down. "I missed you, Bea."

"I missed you too."

I lean down and touch her lips with mine. Her heels bring her up a few inches, so my trek down to her pretty mouth takes me no time at all. That familiar zing hits me as soon as we touch, but when I slide my tongue over her bottom lip, that zing turns into electric shock. She opens her mouth as she wraps her arms around my neck. I slide my hands down to cup her luscious ass, pressing her body into mine. I'm so fucking hard I could cut glass with my dick. "I want you," I say with a husky voice.

She wriggles in my arms, pressing her upper body into me. I can't feel her nipples like I usually do. As I move my mouth down to her neck, kissing and nibbling as I go, I also start to bunch up the bottom of her tight dress. "You smell so good."

Her response is a moan, but she pulls back. "We need to stop. People are watching."

"So? I don't give two fucks. What happens in Vegas stays in Vegas."

"I care." She pulls away from me further, using her hands to push me away to straighten out her dress. "Let's go play some more games."

I adjust my hard-on in my pants and sigh, resigned. "Fine. Let's gamble."

CHAPTER TWENTY

BEA

I wake up to a bright light shining in my eyes. I reach for a blanket but can't seem to find one. I sit up in bed and wince. "Ouch." Pain. My head hurts. Heck, my entire body hurts. I look down at my naked body and wince again. When I glance around the room, it hits me. "This isn't my room." Where the hell am I? Where are my clothes? I roll onto my stomach and peek over the side of the bed and spy my black dress on the floor of what looks like a sunken living room. *A living room?* The room I had before was a standard room with two queen beds, a mini-fridge, and a desk. There was definitely no living room.

I push myself back up to sitting and take a good look around me. The room, or the suite I should say, is ginormous. Taking a slow three-hundred-and-sixty-degree view, my mouth falls wide open. I think a little drool just escaped my mouth. The bed I'm in is massive. There's room for four people in this thing. The bedding and furniture in the room is all soft gold and aubergine. There are touches of white and cream throughout. Running my hand over the sheets, they're cool and soft. No doubt they're a gazillion thread-count. I turn and see the padded headboard. A flashback of last night hits me like a ton of bricks. My face heats with the memory of me holding onto that headboard while Ed is behind me doing amazing things to my body. A chill runs through me from head to toe, making my nipples hard on the way. "Ed." Ed was here with me? But where is he now?

Sliding off the bed, I step onto the plush carpet the shade of a sandy beach and take the two short steps down into the living room. It's decorated in the same color scheme as the bedroom with eggplant-colored chairs in velvet, a yellow-gold couch in a brocade pattern, and a huge glass coffee table trimmed in ornate gold ironwork. Slowly turning in a circle again, I get a complete view of the suite. Just off the living room is another sitting area with a desk complete with a computer and some sort of printer and fax machine. "Wow. This place is amazing."

The light from the floor-to-ceiling windows reminds me that my brain feels like it may explode. I walk to draw the curtains closed and gasp at the view. From the window and this floor, I can see the entire Las Vegas Strip. If I had to guess, I'd say this room was near the top of the hotel. I just don't get it. How did I get here? Pushing the drapes shut most of the way, I sigh with relief as the room falls into semidarkness. I move toward my dress and see my suitcase sitting near the front door. "How did *that* get here?"

I walk to my suitcase and reach out with my left hand to pick it up. That's when I see it. The ring. I quickly look back into the room. I look right and see a set of double doors. Curious, I leave the suitcase and tiptoe, still naked, to the set of double doors. I knock lightly. Maybe Ed's in here. Nothing. I knock again. Still nothing. I turn the doorknob and slowly push it open to reveal the world's largest bathroom. "Holy shit." It's like a bathroom fit for a king. Everything is the same buttery gold color with touches of burnt orange, black, and brushed nickel. There are two sinks, of course. *Double the work for the cleaning crew.* There's a bathtub the size of a hot tub and a walk-in shower

CHAPTER 20

with, I count, "One, two, three, four, five, six showerheads. Wow." There's one more door in this room. I knock. When no one responds, I turn the knob to reveal a separate toilet room. Nope. No Ed.

With my head pounding like a drum corps is living inside, I walk back to the bedroom and sit on the bed, resting my head in my hands. "Think, Beatrice, think." What happened last night? I can't seem to remember anything. Flopping back onto the bed, nausea and the headache rear its ugly head. Jumping up, I race to the bathroom in the nick of time. I wretch so hard, spots float above my head. "I'm *never* drinking again," I mumble between bouts of nausea.

When my body is free of toxins, I feel a little better. I also have an idea. Crawling back out to the desk, I pick up the phone and dial the front desk. Without saying a word, a man speaks. "Yes, Mrs. Flynn. What can I do for you?"

"Mrs. Flynn?"

He chuckles. "Yes, ma'am."

"How did I get moved to this room?" I say, pointing out into the living area. Stupid since he can't see what I'm doing, and thank goodness for that. I'm still naked as a jaybird.

"It's the honeymoon suite and complimentary for our high rollers, Mrs. Flynn."

God, stop calling me that. "Okay. Thanks." I hang up and look down at my hand again. Nope. Not just any ring. This ring is huge with a yellow diamond shaped like a pear surrounded by more diamonds. I bring it closer to my face. Yep, it's a wedding ring. "Now, the big question? Where's my husband?"

CHAPTER TWENTY-ONE

ED

"What the hell have I done?" I mutter as I look down at the Certificate of Marriage I found in my wallet when I was paying for my flight back to Chicago. I've got my ticket in my hand and my seat at the gate waiting for my flight to board. "Why?" I guess that's the universal question. Why did I fly to Vegas in the first place? Why did I stalk Bea like a creep? Why did I drink so much I don't actually remember my own fucking wedding? Why don't I remember our night in our honeymoon bed? Wait, I do remember parts of that. If I weren't so fucking hungover, the memory of her riding me like a rodeo queen would make my dick hard, but I am, and it's not.

"Jesus, Ed. What the fuck have you done?"

CHAPTER TWENTY-TWO

BEA

The minute I discover the receipt from Tiffany's sitting on an end table in the living room, I search the entire suite for the ring box. From the details printed on the form, there seems to be two rings for me and one for Ed. I'm only wearing the humongous yellow one. I hope I haven't lost the other one. Crap, the little one was almost thirty-five-hundred dollars. I need to return this thing; there's no way I can keep it.

TIFFANY & CO.

SALES RECEIPT

PAYMENT METHOD			CUSTOMER		
Cash			Edward Flynn		

QTY	ITEM #	DESCRIPTION	UNIT PRICE	SIZE	LINE TOTAL
1	E1374	Tiffany Soleste® Yellow Pear .5c Platinum	$7,400.00	7.5	$7,400.00
1	W1375	360 Circle Band Ring .33c Platinum	$3,425.00	7.5	$3,425.00
1	B743	Flat Double Milgrain Wedding Band Platinum	$2,325.00	13	$2,325.00

TOTAL DISCOUNT		
	SUBTOTAL	$13,175.00
	SALES TAX	$1,296.69
	TOTAL	$16,671.69

THANK YOU FOR YOUR BUSINESS!

Staring at the receipt for the fifth time, I'm gobsmacked. I can't believe he spent this kind of money on me. Over ten grand for a set of wedding rings? Another two and a half thousand for his ring? *Who does that?* I'm not a ginormous diamond ring kind of girl. Nope. I'm more of a one-hundred-and-fifty-dollar cubic zirconia kind of gal. Why would he do this? How could I *let* him do it? We barely know each other. This all happened thanks to someone named Jameson and another someone called Long Island lemonade. "Uh-oh." Just the thought of the drinks makes me want to hurl.

I gather myself and continue my search for a ring box. When I find nothing on top of any of the tabletop surfaces in the suite, I take to the floor. Crawling on my hands and knees, I look under the bed, the dresser, and the nightstands. Then, I crawl into the living room and spy something small and cube-like under the sofa. "Ah-ha!" I shout and regret it. Oh, shit, my head. At least I found one small Tiffany-blue box. I open the box and gasp in relief. Inside sits one of the other rings. I assume it's the Circle Band ring. "This is so pretty." I pull off the yellow monstrosity, replacing it with the smaller ring. I slide the little diamond band on in its place.

I set the box on top of the receipt and head toward the bathroom. "Shower, dress, and...." It hits me. I look at the clock on one of the tables. "Oh, shit, my interview." I've got precisely twenty minutes before the car the Vegas Knights are sending me arrives to take me to their facility. I wish I didn't have to go, but I can't back out now. It'd be unprofessional. I know I don't want to take the job, not now—not when so much is floating up in the air like a deep, dark storm cloud. But I have to go through with it. I'll just feign interest in the job.

CHAPTER 22

AS SOON AS the tour and my interview are over, I shake hands and thank the Knights for the opportunity. The truth is, I liked everyone there. I felt comfortable—at ease. Even Kent was on his best behavior. Not only that, I got to meet a couple of rookie players who were practicing out on the ice. If they offer me the job, I'll have to give it serious consideration. I don't know what's going to happen with Ed and me, well, except that we won't be married for very long. Hell, he's probably already working on annulment papers.

I ask the driver to drop me off at Tiffany's on the strip. I'm going to cross my fingers that they'll let me return these rings. It's a shame, I really like the small diamond wedding band. It's dainty and sweet. I could picture myself wearing it just because it's pretty—not because it holds any significance. I thank the driver and jump out of the car to walk the half block to the store. Stopping at the door, I push my shoulders back, lift my chin, and step into the fancy-schmancy shop.

"May I help you?" says a man about my age. He's wearing a sleek gray suit and a Tiffany-blue bow tie. Dapper.

"Yes, um, well, I need to return something."

"Oh?" he says with an arched brow.

Instead of speaking, I reach into my purse and pull out the box and receipt. "Yes, we...." I bite my nail. "We were drinking and...."

"You were going to get married on a whim?" He chuckles. "It's Vegas. It happens all the time." He takes the box from my hand and opens it. Whistling, he adds, "Wow, you two went all out, didn't you?"

"We did."

"Okay, let's take a look at your receipt," the well-dressed salesman says as he steps behind one of the glass cases. "This is no problem."

I let out the biggest gust of air with the news. "We'll just need to get Edward in here to sign off on this."

"Edward?"

"The person who bought the rings." He points to Ed's name on the slip.

"He's... he's gone."

"Oh, well, that's unfortunate. I can't return this for you without his signature."

The heat of anxiety and embarrassment over everything that's happened in the last twenty-four hours is rising up from my chest to my neck, I can feel it.

"Oh, dear, now look. You've got thirty days to return these to any Tiffany and Co. in the country. Will you see him in the next month?"

I shrug. "I don't know."

"Keep the receipt and the ring. If you can get in touch with him, he can take care of the return. Okay, sweetie?"

I nod, because if I speak, I won't be able to keep the quiver in my voice at bay. I nod again, picking up the box and sales receipt. I turn and wave to him as I leave. The second I'm on the street, I let it all go. Everything, all of the emotions I've been holding in all day are finally flowing out of me in torrents. How could he do this to me? How could he say all those things last night before, during, and after the wedding? The night has been coming back to me in pieces since I woke up. I've started to recall moments. From the second he stepped up to the blackjack table to the last time he made love to me in our honeymoon bed. How? How could he just leave me? He told me he loved me, and I believed him. God, I'm such a fool.

CHAPTER TWENTY-THREE

BEA: TWO WEEKS LATER

Fall is already upon us here in the Windy City, and that only means one thing... preseason hockey has started. Okay, sure, it means the start of lots of other things, like school, football season, the changing of the leaves from green to shades of red, yellow, and brown. What I meant to say was, for me, it means working fewer banquets and doing more sitting in the stands behind the Blackhawks bench at the United Center. That's where I am right now, watching my hometown team play the Detroit Red Wings in their preseason home opener.

I guess you've figured out that I didn't take the job in Las Vegas. Okay, confession. I may have accepted the job if they'd offered it to me, but they didn't really think they needed my kind of statistical analysis for their inaugural season. No one believes the Knights will win much their first year, so they didn't think they'd need me. The Knights gave me the standard response of they really liked me, but I wasn't a fit. Blah, blah, blah. And that they'd keep my resume on file, so I guess that's something. Truthfully, I wasn't going to take the job anyway. So, back to work with the Blackhawks I go.

The stands are full. Even though it doesn't count toward

each team's season wins and losses, a preseason professional hockey game still draws thousands of people. No matter, it's still exciting and less expensive to watch than a regular season matchup. It's a fantastic atmosphere. I feel lucky to be a part of it. As I watch Patrick Kane speed down the ice toward the Red Wing's net, I feel a tap on my shoulder. I turn and blink at a tiny woman. She looks familiar. Dang, I know I should know this woman. *But from where?* I blink again.

"Bea? You may not remember me, but I'm Sarah Flynn. Ed's aunt."

Shit. "Oh, right." I turn in my seat to shake her hand. "It's nice to see you again." I quickly scan the crowd around her, looking for Ed. Or maybe I'm making sure he's not here. I don't think I could face him.

"So, are you doing your statistics now?" she says, pointing down to my pad of paper and pen. I've also got a laptop open on the floor in front of my feet for data entry.

"Yes. I do general statistics during the game. I'll have to watch the game film to do more of the in-depth stuff." Why am I telling her all of that? She doesn't care.

"You must be quite a math whiz."

I shrug. "It's hereditary. My dad teaches computational complexity theory, algorithms, and combinatorics at the University of Chicago."

"Wow, I don't know what any of that means." Sarah giggles. "I guess you do come by it naturally."

Not knowing what to say anymore, I tap my pencil nervously on my leg. I look back at the game and see I've missed at least one shot on goal. It's okay, I always watch game film to go over everything anyway.

"Well, I don't want to keep you from your important work. I should get back to my seat. I've got to admit, Bea, I haven't the foggiest clue what's going on at this game. My husband drug me here along with another couple. He seems to like when they fight." She rolls her eyes. "*Men.*"

"Oh, right. Yeah, I can see that." The truth is, fights are part of game strategy. And, I love the fights, most people do, but I'm not going to admit that to Sarah right now. "Good to see you, Sarah."

"You too, sweetie." She turns to leave then stops. "Hey! What are you doing tomorrow?"

"Tomorrow?"

"Yeah. Sunday. Tomorrow."

Crap, I can't think of a thing I'm doing. Before I can make up something, Sarah continues, "Because I'm having brunch with Emily and Sandy. They can't stop talking about you after the party at The Galway Arms. They'd love to see you again. Will you come?"

"Oh, I—"

"Please?" she says, smiling sweetly.

I nod. "Sure." I tear off a corner of a sheet of paper and jot down my number. "Can you text me with the time and place?"

"Of course!" she says, sounding giddy. "The girls are going to flip!"

Flip? "It'll be fun to see them again too." Oh, crud. What have I done?

"See you tomorrow." Sarah practically skips up the steps to the mezzanine level. I watch her turn right and off into the crowd. It's no wonder everyone is milling about; the first period is now over, and it's off to concessions or the bathroom en masse.

"What have I done?" I thought I was through with Ed Flynn. Okay, I'm still through with him, but this is going to make all of that with him super awkward. What if he finds out I'm lunching with his aunt and cousins? He's not going to like it. I'm not sure I blame him.

AT TWELVE ON SUNDAY, I find myself pacing on the sidewalk in front of Mrs. Murphy and Sons Irish Bistro. It's not that I'm nervous to enter Mrs. M's. I'm not. I've been here many times. My mom loves this place. It's just that I don't know what I'm walking into with Sarah, Emily, and Sandy Flynn. What if they ask me questions about Ed? "Shit. What if they know about Vegas?" Surely Ed wouldn't have told anyone. "God, I hope not." What if they invited me to interrogate me—to make me feel like crap about everything?

I roll my eyes and yank the door open. Might as well get this done. I step into the dark interior and scan the room. I hear my name before I see them. My eyes follow the sound to a large round table filled with women. Flynn women. I smile weakly and make my way toward them, muttering to myself, "What the hell was I thinking?" I thought she said it was going to be just the three of them. "Damn it. I should have gotten out of this." Gathering my resolve, I step up to the table and smile. Touching the only empty seat, I ask, "Is this seat taken?"

"No!" shouts Emily from across the table. "It's yours, babe."

I pull the chair out and sit as Sarah asks, "Bea? Have you met everyone?"

I shake my head. "Only Emily and Sandy." I look at a woman with bluish hair. "Oh, wait. I worked at your wedding, right?"

"Yep. I'm Claire. I married Ethan. Ed's baby brother." Claire reaches out to shake my hand.

"I'm Kennedy." A gorgeous redhead reaches out to shake next. "I'm dating Ernie, Ed's middle brother."

"Married to—not dating," corrects Claire with an eye roll.

Kennedy rolls her eyes. "Don't remind me."

Everyone laughs, and I only smile. I don't get the joke. I guess I'd have to know something about Ed's brother to get it.

She shrugs. "It's new. We just got married last weekend," explains Kennedy.

As I wait for more information, our server approaches to get our drink orders. Four of the women order some kind of alcoholic beverage while Kennedy orders a rose lemonade. Since I swore off booze in Vegas, I'm going with Kennedy and ordering Rocky's ginger beer. As we wait for our drinks, I sit quietly, listening to the women banter. They're a lively bunch, and several times I catch myself giggling about some story about one of the Flynns.

I'm caught off guard when Sarah asks, "So, what do you think of all of our unruly Flynn men?"

"Unruly? I didn't notice that. I couldn't get past the idea that they were the hottest humans I've ever seen in my entire life. You all could sell your DNA. People would line up for miles for some of that stuff like they do for thoroughbred horses." I watch the women's faces and regret saying a damn word. Their mouths are agape. When Sandy starts giggling, it doesn't take long for Emily to start too. In no time, the entire table is lost in a fit of laughter. They're so loud they're drawing attention from some of the other patrons. It's contagious, though. I start to laugh too.

"Oh, shit, girl. That was fucking hilarious. Please do *not* tell any of the guys that. They've all got fat heads already," says Sandy once she calms down. "But, fuck, that was funny. Who knew you were so hilarious, Bea?"

"Language, Sandy," says Sarah curtly. Turning to me, she rolls her eyes. "Forgive my daughter. She's got a terrible mouth."

I shrug. "No worries." Besides, I can be funny. I just wasn't trying to be funny then. No joke. The Flynns could rake in millions.

Everyone calms down once our brunch orders are in, and I

can't wait to eat. I'm hungry today, which is nice since my appetite has been kind of spotty lately. Eating soon also means I can leave as soon as we're fed. I like these ladies. They're very nice. I just don't feel comfortable befriending them when it's just going to end badly. I'm lost in thought when I hear Sandy. "Wow, that's a beautiful ring, Bea. Where'd you get it?"

I look down at the diamond band on my left ring finger. "Oh, this?" I hold up my finger. "Las Vegas." I took to wearing the diamond band when I came back home. I'll pay Ed back for it if I ever see him again.

"Las Vegas?" asks Emily. "Ed just got back from Las Vegas. Did you two go together?"

I'm not lying when I respond, "No. We didn't go together."

"Well, it's a gorgeous ring. Can I see it?" Sandy has her palm out to me. Without thinking, I pull it off my finger and set it in her palm. Sandy looks at it closely and smiles. "Tiffany's?"

"Yes. How did you know?"

"It's stamped right here on the inside of the band." I never noticed that before. Probably because I haven't taken it off since that day in the hotel room.

"Can I see it?" asks Sarah. Sandy passes it to Claire who glances at it briefly. She passes it to Kennedy who does the same. Emily holds it next, then it finally lands in Sarah's hand. She brings it up toward her eyes and moves it back and forth, making it sparkle. "Well, it's a lovely wedding band."

"Uh...."

"A wedding band?" asks Claire. She turns to me. "Is it a wedding band?"

"Bea?" asks Emily. "Did you get hitched in Vegas?" She snickers. "Spill, girl! Who is he? Do we know him?"

"Yeah, who is he?" asks Sandy.

The questions are being thrown at me so fast I don't have time to respond to any of them. I feel bile rising up from my stomach thanks to the barrage of questions. Without saying a word, I stand up quickly. "I, uh, need to go to the ladies' room." I turn and walk briskly to the restroom. Luckily, no one is using the single bathroom unit, so I open the door and throw myself toward the toilet just as I lose the only thing in my stomach, ginger beer. "Yuck." It doesn't taste very good coming back up.

"Beatrice?"

Damn, I didn't lock the door.

"Honey, can I come in?"

"Sure, Sarah."

"Are you okay, honey?" She's next to me, using her hand to push the hair back from my face. I bet she's a great mom.

"Yeah. It just hit me all of a sudden." That's the truth.

"I'm sorry if we upset you back there. The girls can be quite overwhelming."

"No, it's fine." I stand up slowly and make my way to the sink to rinse my mouth.

"Can I ask you something?"

Like I'm going to say no. "Sure."

"Did Ed give you this ring?"

"Um." I look down at my hands as I swirl soap around in my palms. When I look into the mirror, our eyes meet. "Yes."

"So, you did go to Vegas with him?"

"No. I was there for a job interview. He surprised me. He showed up out of the blue."

"And you were married there?"

I nod. "We gambled and drank—a lot. Then we went to Tiffany's on the way to one of the wedding chapels."

"So, are you living with Ed now?"

I look over at her and blink. "No."

"Why not?"

I blink at her again. "Because... um, because...." I choke. "I woke up in our hotel room, and he was gone." I squeeze my eyes closed, willing back the threat of tears. Geesh, I've been so emotional lately. "I haven't seen or heard from him in two weeks."

"Excuse me?" she barks.

Is she mad at me? "Sarah, it wasn't my fault...." I turn away from her and cover my face with my hands. I feel nausea hit me suddenly and barely make it to the toilet before I lose the little that's left in my stomach. It's mostly dry heaves at this point. I sit back on my heels and look up to see Sarah above me. "It's not my fault, Sarah. H-He l-left me."

"Oh, honey." Sarah kneels in front of me and wraps her arms around me. "I didn't mean to sound angry with you. It's Ed I'm angry with right now."

"M-Me too. He told me he l-l-loved me."

"I'm sure he does, angel. Ed's just confused."

I pull back from her hug to respond angrily. "I'm the one that should be confused."

"Of course, Bea. Come on. Let's get you cleaned up. Then, I need to tell you a story that may help you understand Ed a little better. Will you let me do that?"

I shrug. "I guess." Pushing myself up to standing, I take a hesitant step. That feeling of nausea isn't completely gone yet. Slowly, I make my way to the sink again. I take my time because I'm not sure I want to hear what Sarah has to say. Whatever it is, I'm sure it'll make me feel something other than rage toward Ed. It's the only way I've been able to function since I flew back. I need anger to survive all of this right now.

CHAPTER TWENTY-FOUR

BEA

After my breakdown in the bathroom, Sarah offered to drive me home. She stopped at the table to tell the other women in our group that I was ill and to eat without us. I didn't even have to show my red, blotchy face again. Thank goodness for that. In the car, Sarah did all of the talking. Another "thank goodness." What she told me was both illuminating and discouraging, but I listened. How could I not? I think Sarah Flynn has a knack for getting people to listen.

I wipe my eyes and blow my nose as I open the door to exit her vehicle. "Thanks for sharing all of that with me, Sarah." I step one foot onto our concrete driveway. "And thanks for telling the girls I had an upset stomach."

"Of course. You did have an upset stomach. Either that or you're pregnant." Sarah doesn't laugh that off like I expect her to.

I stop myself from getting out of the car. "Oh, I'm not pregnant." There's no way.

"Are you sure?"

"Yes." I pause. "I'm 95 percent sure."

She raised one eyebrow. "The Flynn men are extremely potent, Bea. Five percent is all they need."

I blink at her again. "I can't." I swallow deeply, hoping I don't need to make a mad dash to the restroom. I start again. "I can't. I have a unicorn uterus."

"A what?"

Starting again, I say, "It's called a unicornuate uterus. My uterus is malformed. It's shaped like a horn and half the size of a normal uterus. There's no room in there to carry a child."

Sarah nods but says nothing.

"My doctor told me I'd never get pregnant. I read up on it, and he wasn't exactly right. There's a slight chance, 5 percent, that I could get pregnant, but then there's only a 47 percent chance a child would survive the pregnancy. So, even if I did miraculously become pregnant, I'll most likely miscarry or have an ectopic pregnancy. I could also deliver way too early, which puts a child at too great a risk."

"Wow. That's terrible, Beatrice." Sarah doesn't smile. "It doesn't rule out the possibility that you're pregnant though, right?"

I shrug. "I guess not."

"Let's do this. Let me drive us to the nearest drugstore. We can pick up a pregnancy test or two. It doesn't hurt to check, does it?"

"No. But I'm not pregnant, Sarah. I've just got a flu bug or something."

"Indulge me, sweetie."

I bring my legs back into the car and shut the door. "Fine."

After the stop at the nearest pharmacy, Sarah pulls into my driveway again. Before I get out of her car, I turn and hug Sarah. "Thank you, Sarah."

"My pleasure, sweetheart."

"Sarah? Please don't say anything to Ed. Don't even tell him you saw me. If I am pregnant, I don't want that to be the reason Ed decides to contact me. I'd rather raise a child alone than be with a man who feels obligated."

"Bea, if you are pregnant, he deserves to know."

"I agree. *If*, and it's a big *if*, I was able to carry the baby to full term and give birth to a baby, I'll let him know. There's no need for both of us to be heartbroken over a lost child. Besides, Ed doesn't want children."

"Oh, of course, he—"

"No." I shake my head. "He was adamant. He said he raised children already. He doesn't want to do it again."

"I told you—"

"I know. I heard everything you said. Let's just take it one thing at a time, please. Promise me this conversation stays between the two of us. Can you do that?"

"Of course. I promise, Bea."

"Thank you. It was nice seeing you again, Sarah."

"You too, Bea."

I shut the car door and walk up to my front door, all the while hoping Sarah keeps her promise. The last thing I want is Ed Flynn at my door because he feels duty bound.

AS I LIE IN BED, I place my hand on my stomach. *Pregnant*. It seems impossible and incredibly scary. My body shivers with excitement and dread. In my heart, I know it won't work out for me. But I need to enjoy this feeling, this idea of a baby. I will have plenty of time to mourn when the inevitable happens. Shaking off those negative thoughts, my mind turns to Sarah and what she told me in the car earlier. Hell, it's all I could think about all day.

"Ed was eleven when Rachel, his mother, died. She was my best friend, Bea," she adds, looking at me with sadness in her eyes. "I loved her like a sister. So, when she was diagnosed with cancer, I was devastated. We were all devastated. By the time they discovered it, Rachel was stage four and very ill. The doctors told her that treatment would only prolong the inevitable and would make her quality of life hell. Ernie and Ethan were both babies, really. So much so Rachel insisted they not know the prognosis. Because Ed was the eldest, but still a baby as far as I was concerned, Donal felt he should know what was happening."

Sarah turns in her seat at the wheel to face me. "Donal was beside himself. He could barely function, but while he tried to stay strong for Rachel, he relied on Ed heavily. Ed became the primary caregiver for Ernie and Ethan. Ed did everything from bathing them and feeding the entire family to making sure the boys did their homework and went to school.

"He was the babysitter, the housekeeper, and a nurse to Rachel. All of us did what we could to help them, but Donal was stubborn. He wanted to pretend he had it under control. He didn't. Ed did." Sarah then reaches up and wipes a tear from her cheek. "I tried to talk to Donal about it, but he was so distraught, I don't think he really heard me. We all watched Rachel wither away, and when the time grew nearer, Donal grew almost despondent. He'd work a few hours a day, but then he'd spend the other twenty-two hours at her bedside. One of those times Donal was at work, she asked to speak to Ed. I was there when she told Ed how much she loved him and how much she appreciated everything he did to help his dad and brothers. Then, she asked him to be there for his dad and baby brothers after... to be the man of the house and to promise her he'd always take care of them. She was counting on him to be strong for the rest of them."

I gasp at that part of the story. "That's a lot to ask an eleven-year-old boy."

"It was. In all honesty, I don't think Rachel meant for Ed to take it to heart like he did. I think she knew Ed was the kind of boy that needed a job to do. But the poor child didn't even have time to mourn. She died two days later, and I don't remember him even shedding a tear. He cared for the boys and his dad like it was his job."

"But his job was to be a boy, not a man."

"It was. Bea, but it's been eighteen years, and Ed never stopped taking care of them. I know he had big dreams when he was a kid. He wanted to see the world. He wanted to go to college to study architecture. But he wasn't able to do any of that."

"He went to college though."

"Yes, he did. Then law school. He hated law school."

I nod. "I see why you told me all of that, Sarah. But it doesn't really explain why he left me in Las Vegas."

"If I had to guess, I'd say he was overwhelmed. He may be afraid of losing you, of going through the pain of losing someone he loves. You'll have to ask Ed about that, honey."

I shrug. "I need to think about this. I'm not sure it helps me understand our situation any better, but I'll think about it."

She pats me on the leg. "You do that. But can you promise me something?"

I say nothing as I wait for her to continue.

"When Ed realizes he wants to be your husband, and he will realize it, will you let him?"

"Sarah—"

"Listen. Ed's a thinker. Every decision he's ever made has come after careful consideration."

I arch my brow. "He decided pretty fast in Vegas."

Sarah chuckles. "I know. That's why I'm positive he'll pull his head out of his you-know-what and show up at your door someday soon. And when he does, please let him explain. Promise me?"

I don't know if I can promise, but I say, "I'll try. I'll listen, but that's all I can promise."

"That's all I can ask for then—for you to hear him out."

I let her words roll around in my head again and sigh, "Poor Ed." I get it. He was forced to grow up at age eleven. He never mourned his mom's death because he had to be strong for everyone else. Ed told me he already raised two kids, and now I see why he feels that way. He did raise two kids, and he cared for the adults in his life at the same time. He's always done the right thing for everyone else.

I guess that means he doesn't have anything left for me. He's all used up inside. I think that's what I saw in his eyes that night at the reception. There was sadness there. I recognized it immediately. But it doesn't change the fact that he hurt me. For some reason, he's able to be strong for everyone. Everyone but me.

CHAPTER TWENTY-FIVE

ED

God, I'm tired. It feels like I haven't slept for a year. In reality, I haven't slept for two weeks and two days. *How can I sleep when all I do is remember?* I remember how she looked the moment she stepped off the elevator in that tight-as-sin black dress and spiked heels. Or her shocked expression when I sat down next to her at the blackjack table. I smile when I think of her mouth in that "O" shape when I won on the megabucks slot machine. I'd only played once. Three bucks gave me a return of forty-five grand in less than thirty seconds. It was my lucky night.

When I picked out the ring at Tiffany's.... I pull open the top drawer of my desk and peer down at the light blue box. Picking it up, I pop open the lid and stare. Her giant yellow ring now sits snuggly against my own wedding band in the same box. Yeah, I remember her expression. I could tell the smile she gave me at the store was forced—she didn't care for the huge thing. It was too big for her dainty hand, but it was yellow, like a bumblebee. I had to get it for her. It's no wonder she sent it back to me with the receipt and a short note telling me I had "twenty-eight days to return it for a full refund."

Shutting the lid, I set the box back into the drawer. Sighing, I lay my head on the back of my chair. Squeezing my eyes closed, I recall how beautiful she was at the Little White Wedding Chapel. Sure, we were drunk. But it felt right. When she said, "I do" and "I love you too," I felt a million feet tall because I was proud to be her husband and proud she was my wife.

God, we had so much fun that night—*all* night. Jesus, the sex was fucking amazing. Hands down the best sex of my goddamn life. She was wild and fucking sexy as she took the lead for part of the night. We did *everything*. She sucked and licked my dick like her life depended on it. I finally got a taste of her, and it was fucking addictive and sweet. But the best part of the night was when she rubbed the chocolate mint from the pillow all over her tiny tits. Jesus, I nearly came just from watching her coat her pink nipples in dark chocolate. "Fuck." I feel my work pants grow tighter the more I think about her. I need to stop. No good will come of it. I left her there like a coward. It's for the best. She deserves much better than me. I'm broken—fucked up.

I lay my head back again and close my eyes. "Sleep. I just need sleep."

"ED?"

I'm so startled by the voice, I jerk back in my office chair, nearly falling backward. Regaining my balance, I look to my open door just as my aunt steps into my office at Flynn Construction. "Aunt Sarah? What're you doing here?"

"I was in the neighborhood."

I stare at her, waiting. She doesn't usually visit the Flynn

CHAPTER 25

Construction offices. "Declan isn't here. He's out at the new site up north."

"Oh, I know." She steps into my office and sits in the chair in front of my desk. "I saw a friend of yours yesterday."

Ah, there it is. I know Sarah well enough to know who she means. I'll play along. "Where did you see her?" I hope Bea isn't ingratiating herself with my family. She'll only get hurt.

"Brunch. I saw her at a hockey game the other night and invited her to brunch with the girls."

Shit. "Aunt Sarah, she shouldn't be—"

"Don't worry, she didn't stay. She got sick to her stomach before the food was served. I drove her home."

"Sick?"

"Sick."

What does that even mean? Why is she telling me this? "I'm sure she's okay."

Sarah shrugs. "Maybe."

I look at Sarah's face and wait. When she doesn't say anything more, I find I can't stand the silence. "Just spit it out, Aunt Sarah."

"I've no idea what you mean, honey."

I roll my eyes. "Say what you came here to say."

She leans forward in her seat. "I love you like you were my own, Ed. You know that, right?"

Oh, shit. Here we go. "I know."

"Do you?"

"Yes." I know.

"Do you remember that day?" She pauses. "The day Rachel—your mom—asked you to be the man in your family?"

Fuck. "Aunt Sarah, I don't want to talk about that."

"It's time we talked about it."

"No, it's not." It'll never be time to talk about that. She died right after that. She fell asleep and never really woke up again. It's the last time I talked to her. Mom knew. She knew it would be the last time. Fuck! "I don't want to fucking talk about it," I growl.

"Language!"

I've never known anyone who hates cussing more than Sarah Flynn. "Sorry."

"I need you to hear me out. Will you do that?"

I nod. I want to say no, but I can't out of respect.

"All right. I'm going to say something that might upset you, Ed. Are you ready to hear it?"

I nod, but I'm not really ready.

"Rachel was wrong."

I tense up at those words. Mom was never wrong. My mom was perfect.

"She should never have told you to 'be the man of the house.' You were eleven."

"Old enough to—"

"Shh, let me finish. I've been holding this in for years." Sarah stands up and walks up to my desk, looking down at me. "I know why she did it. She did it so her death wouldn't destroy you. She didn't mean it the way you took it, though. You were a child...."

I run my hands over my face to regroup. I remain silent.

"She did it to give you something to occupy your mind. You've always been very determined and goal-oriented. But here's the problem, Ed. You took the responsibility too far, too literally. She didn't mean for you to do it forever. Just long enough for you to get past your grief."

"With all due respect, Aunt Sarah, you know nothing about this."

"Excuse me?" Sarah retorts. "I was the only other adult in the room that day. After you left the room, she looked at me and said,

'Help him get over this, Sarah. Of all of my boys, Ed's the most sensitive. He'll mourn for too long. He'll be angry and become withdrawn. Being responsible for his family will help him cope.'"

"She did *not* say that."

"Edward Declan Flynn, I'm going to ignore that comment. I'd never lie to you about your mom. I loved her too," she says, her voice becoming soft and shaky.

"I know. I'm sorry. I just meant...."

Sarah walks around to my side of the desk and places her hand on my shoulder. "Stop thinking you have to be responsible for your family and start thinking about yourself, your own life. Isn't it time you found a way to be happy? Your dad and brothers are fine. You did an amazing job with all of them. It's because of you that your siblings are happy—successful. You've got permission to be selfish now."

I snort because I'm the most selfish asshole I know. If she only knew.... Fuck, maybe she does. "Did Bea say anything to you?"

She shrugs. "I'll never tell you what we talked about, Ed. So, you've got two choices."

"Two choices?"

"Yep. You could sit here and stew about what Bea and I talked about, or you can call her and ask her yourself."

"I'm not calling her."

"Oh, good idea. Go see Bea instead." She turns and walks around my desk, picking up her purse as she goes.

"Aunt Sarah?"

"Yes?"

"It's over between Bea and me. It's for the best."

Turning to face me, she spits. "Bullshit."

The woman who never cusses just let one fly. It makes me smile. "Language, Aunt Sarah."

"I'm only going to tell you this once, Ed. Go see her or you may live to regret it."

"Jesus." I run my hand through my hair. "What the hell did she say?"

She shrugs. "Your mom would have loved Bea."

"Don't go there," I reply bitterly.

"Oh, I went there. Rachel would have loved her, and do you want to know why?"

No. Sighing, I acquiesce. "Why?"

"Because Bea loves you in spite of your shortcomings. What mother wouldn't want that for their favorite child."

She still loves me? "Favorite child? I wasn't her favorite."

Sarah lifts one brow at me and steps out of my office.

I wasn't her favorite. Mom didn't play favorites. She loved us all equally.

"Go see your wife, Ed," I hear her shout from the hallway.

Fuck! I knew it. Bea told the one person in my family who can't keep her mouth shut. "My wife? So you know?" I shout back.

Poking her face back through my doorway, she says, "Yes. She didn't want to tell me, but I drug it out of her."

"Does anyone else know?" Aunt Sarah can't keep a secret to save a life.

"No. No one else knows. I promised Bea I wouldn't tell anyone. I also promised I wouldn't talk to you, but I couldn't let that one stand. I can and will keep my promise about your marriage."

I arch a brow at her this time.

"I can keep a secret. You've no idea the secrets I've kept, young man."

"Please, just don't say a word to anyone."

I watch as my aunt disappears into the hallway again. I love my aunt; I know she means well, but this time, she's wrong. Bea is never going to forgive me, and that's for the best. I suspect Bea feels the same since she sent me back the ring. Hell, I've been expecting annulment papers from her every single day. If I don't get those soon, I'll draw some up myself, because what happened in Vegas should probably stay there.

CHAPTER TWENTY-SIX

ED: TWO WEEKS LATER

When my crew decided they wanted to go out somewhere to celebrate the *almost*-end to our job, I came up with the idea of going to the Blackhawk's final home preseason hockey game. Sure, I know Bea works for them. It's why I chose this place for our outing. The odds I'll actually see her are pretty slim, however. She probably works up in one of the private areas in the arena. My aunt saw her here, so there's a chance she could find her way down by the team bench. I slide my hand into my right jean pocket and run the contents between my fingers. Nervous habit today, I guess.

Even if I don't spot her, I'm really here to thank my crew for a job well done on the home renovation. We're completely finished with all of the exterior work, including the roof, new windows, gutters, and siding. We've built a detached two-car garage on the property and prepped the yard for new landscaping. All the interior needs is to finish carpentry and some painting. I wish I could tell you I was consistently hands-on on that project, but I've been a worthless piece of shit for the last month. So, getting tickets to a pro sporting event is the least I could do.

Once all twelve guys are seated, I hand each of them fifty

bucks. "Go get some beer and food on me." I hear a collective "hell yeah" from my crew as they all file out to get grub before they drop the first puck. I get comfortable in my seat as the teams warm up down on the ice. It's a fascinating game to watch. It's sort of a combination of basketball—the way they race back and forth on the ice and attempt to shoot a puck into a net, except these guys have to fly around on thin metal blades on ice —combine that with baseball, soccer, and some football thanks to the hits and brawls that happen now and then. It's a sport that requires many skills from the players.

My eyes are trained on the Blackhawk's side of the ice. They're running shooting drills, batting the puck back and forth, and attempting to get it around their own goalie without much success—Corey Crawford is a stellar goaltender. I scan from our goalie to the home team's bench and start to look to the Bruin's side when I spot her. Bea. My breath stops for a second. It's been a month since I last saw her. It feels like a year thanks to my insomnia. I can't seem to sleep anymore.

I slump down in my seat a bit, hoping she doesn't spot me. I just wanted to see her. I'm up high enough and there are enough people in the stands now, I should be plenty obscured. I don't stop looking at her though. She's holding a notebook in one hand and has a laptop open on her lap. She's sitting on the bench talking to one of the players. His jersey says number two. I grab the program that I bought when I came into the United Center, turning to the page with the player roster. I search for number two. "Duncan Keith." I look back down at Bea and Keith. He's sitting too fucking close to her. He's leaning in so much, apparently looking at her notebook, but I don't buy it. I watch as he points to something on her computer; he speaks, and she laughs. She fucking throws her head back and laughs like he's the funniest fucking asshole in the entire world. I crumple the program in my hand until it's a wrinkled wad of paper. Tossing it to the ground, I run my fingers through my hair. "Stop it, Ed. She's just doing her job."

I look back down at her because I'm a glutton for punishment, I guess. Keith is no longer sitting next to her. Now it's number ten. I reach down and uncurl the program. The guy that's standing behind her with one big palm on her shoulder and his face pressed against her head is "Patrick *fucking* Sharp." As he points to something on her open computer screen, Bea is talking like she's explaining something to him. When she's finished speaking, the fucking dick leans down and kisses her cheek. He. Kisses. *My*. Wife's. Fucking. Cheek. I watch her face turn pink. She's blushing? *Jesus. Does she have a thing for that asshole?*

I can't wrap my head around all of this jealousy. This time, I rip the fucking program in half and toss it to the ground. I stand up and march up the steps to the mezzanine then out the door to the concourse, taking a right. I walk past the guys getting beers and food and past the stand that sells novelty items. I move beyond the twenty beer stands and double that number in food kiosks. I keep walking until I reach the other side of the arena. When I find an opening, I turn right and head down the steps, moving in the direction of the Blackhawk's bench.

The game hasn't started yet, so I guess that's why no one has tried to stop me. I kind of wish someone would. When I go as far as I can, I'm stopped by the tall Plexiglas that surrounds the team bench. Bea is still going over something with yet another player. I raise my fist and hit the glass, hard. I get the attention of a trainer or some shit. When we make eye contact, I point to Bea. The guy taps her on the shoulder and points to me. When she sees me, that pretty blush she had is gone, leaving her ghost white.

Her eyelashes flutter in confusion as her mouth forms the words "What are you doing here?"

I can't hear her due to the thick glass between us and all of the noise that's surrounding us on the ice and off, so I just stand in my spot and stare at her. She's so beautiful tonight in her simple red Blackhawks T-shirt. Her hair is a wild mess piled on top of her head. There are tendrils falling down on either side of her face. Why did I ever think that wasn't pretty?

Fuck. I don't know if I can do what I came to do now that I'm here. I should just turn around and go back to my seat and forget I ever saw her. But there's a part of me that wants to drag her away from those hockey assholes and take her somewhere private. Goddamn, I miss her. How did this happen? Before I met Bea, I was happy. Okay, happy is probably too strong a word. All I know is, since I met her, my life has been a roller coaster of emotions.

Without another thought, I start to turn around, but I'm stopped when I hear her. "Ed?"

I turn back to see Bea coming out of a small doorway at the end of the bench. I don't respond. I merely stare. She's lost weight. I did that to her. *Fuck.*

"What are you doing here?"

"I came to see a game. Why else would I be here?" *Why did I say that?* I can't seem to fucking help myself—I can't stop being an asshole to her.

"Oh, right. I'm sorry."

She steps back inside the door, but I stop her. "No. Wait."

She hesitates but doesn't move closer to me. "What do you want?"

"I, uh, I saw you and just thought I'd say hello." I run a palm over my right jean pocket.

"Sure. Okay. Hello to you too."

Before she can run away, I say, "You look beautiful, Bea."

"Ed, this isn't a good idea."

"It's a bad idea to say you look beautiful?" Hell, I finally said something nice, and she doesn't like it?

"Yes. No. Well, any of this." She looks down at the floor. "Can you hang on a second? I've got something for you."

"Sure."

I watch her walk over to her seat. She picks up her purse and reaches a hand inside. When she brings her hand back out, she's holding a large yellow envelope. Back through the doorway, she makes her way to me. "Here."

"What's this?" The envelope has my name and address written on it. There are stamps as well. She was going to mail this to me.

"Papers. I need you to sign them and mail them back to me. There's a self-addressed envelope in there for you. All right?"

I watch her turn away from me. "That's it?"

She turns her pretty face back to me, and I see tears. "Yes. That's it. Now, I need to get back to work. Goodbye, Ed."

Goodbye? The way she said it made it sound so final. "Goodbye?"

She nods and walks back into the bench area. It's now swarming with hulking, sweaty hockey dudes. A few of them look first at her, then at me. They look pissed. No doubt they think I made her cry. They'd be right. How many times has it been now? Five? Six? I've lost count of the number of times I've hurt my girl—my *wife*. I should tell her I'm not worth crying about, but something tells me she's already figured that out.

As I turn to leave, I rip open the envelope and read the first line of text:

Summons And Petition For Annulment: (No Minor Children)

After reading those words, I feel my heartbeat increase. It's thumping so hard I think it may pound right out of my chest. My throat is getting tight, and my eyes are starting to burn. Heat is rising up from my chest onto my face. I feel angry—anxious—sad. Why does she want to end our marriage now? Is she seeing someone else?

I crumple the papers and the envelope in my hand and look at the bench, making eye contact with her. I use both hands to press the pages into a tight ball. Shaking my head, I turn and walk up the steps to the mezzanine. An annulment? It's what I thought I wanted after I got back from Vegas, but it's not how I feel now. Now I don't want an annulment, but I don't think it's a decision I get to make or even participate in anymore—Bea's already decided. "Fuck!" I mutter as I walk back to my seat. I look down at the manila envelope in my hand. I want to throw it the fuck away, but that's not being fair to her.

Back in my seat, I throw a fake smile at my crew who all seem to be having a good time. The game started between the time I left Bea and got back to my crew. Back in my seat, I scan the Blackhawk's bench but don't see her. I look left and right of the bench and then spot her. She's sitting behind the team, laptop open on her lap. "God, she's so fucking pretty," I murmur to myself.

"Who's fucking pretty?" asks my plumber, Bill.

"Nobody, dude. Nobody." I slap him on the back and turn to watch the game, all the while keeping an eye on my wife.

CHAPTER TWENTY-SEVEN

BEA

Seeing Ed at the hockey game was unexpected and unnerving. I can't believe I had the wherewithal to give him the annulment papers. I half expected him to ask for a pen. Instead, he crumpled the papers up and walked away. For a second, I felt a glimmer of hope he'd pull me into his arms and tell me he loves me and that he was the biggest jerk in the entire world and that he wants to be a family. Alas, that didn't happen. No doubt he just needs to take the papers home so he can read them in attorney-mode. He probably wants to make sure I'm not trying to take him to the cleaners. I'm not. I don't want a thing from him. *Nothing but him.*

God, he looked perfect in his flannel shirt, gray tee, and jeans. The tee was just snug enough to fit tightly against his abdomen, and his jeans were low-slung and snug over his thighs. The man is gorgeous. The minute I saw him, my breath left me as I placed my hand on my stomach. For a split second, I thought he came about the baby, but that's impossible. He doesn't know about that. No one does. Not even my mom. It's not like I don't want my mom and dad to know, it's just I don't want them to be sad when the time comes. They are loving and emotional people. If they knew they'd lost a grandchild, it would devastate them.

I went to see my regular doctor for a pregnancy test; it was positive, same as the home tests. He referred me to an obstetrician at the University of Chicago who specializes in high-risk pregnancies. I met with her last week. So far, there are no red flags, but it's early. I'm four weeks along now, and it's been a rough four weeks. I've spent most of that time worshipping the porcelain goddess. I seem to feel better in the mornings than I do in the afternoon and evenings. Dr. Jargon assures me things are fine but that I need to take it easy. She recommended I stop waiting tables if at all possible. It's possible. She wasn't concerned about this job with the Hawks, not yet anyway. Thank goodness.

As the game progresses, I find myself scanning the crowd. I don't want to see him again, but I can't seem to help myself. I concentrate on the areas in front of me since turning around to skim the crowd would be awkward. On my fifth or sixth pass, I see him. Unfortunately, he sees me too. Our eyes meet, and I force myself to look back down at my laptop. When I look up again, he's still staring at me. I give him a weak smile, and he gives me one back. I feel my stomach flip angrily, and I know what's coming. I quickly stand juggling my laptop and papers. I excuse myself, walking sideways down the row I'm in to get to the steps. My experience has told me I've got about a minute before I lose the saltines I ate for supper. I stomp up the steps and just as I get to the mezzanine, I race to the nearest trash receptacle and do the unthinkable. That's right, ladies and gents, I lost my crackers. So disgusting.

CHAPTER TWENTY-EIGHT

ED

"What the fuck?" I mutter as I lean forward in my seat. Did Bea just yack in a trash can? I jump up.

"Boss?"

I look down at Bill. "Back in a second." I run up the steps and keep running all the way around the concourse until I get to the same entrance I took half an hour ago. Just as I'm about to jog down the steps, I nearly run into someone. It's her. "Bea? Are you okay?" She looks like shit. She's pale and shaky. "Bea?"

"Oh, hey, Ed. Yeah, just have an upset stomach."

"Are you sure? Do you need me to take you to the hospital? I can drive you home."

She chuckles. "No. I'm fine. If I need anything, I'll just go to one of the trainers."

"You shouldn't be here, Bea, if you've got the flu or something. Think of other people, at least."

She looks up at me with hurt in her eyes. I know I fucking said the wrong thing again.

"No worries. You can't catch what I've got." She walks around me and out into the main hallway.

"What's that supposed to mean? Are you on antibiotics?"

"Sure. Yeah." She walks into the ladies' restroom without another look back at me.

Why? Why do I say the wrong things all the damn time? I lean against the wall and wait. And wait. "What the hell is taking so long?"

When a woman walks past me to enter the bathroom, I stop her, "Ma'am? Can you do me a favor?"

She looks hesitant. "Uh, sure."

"When you get in there, can you ask for Beatrice? She's been in there a while. I need to make sure she's okay."

The woman nods and enters the bathroom. I hear her say Bea's name several times. Then I hear "Oh, dear." Her footsteps sound hurried and are getting louder the closer they get to me. "Hey, if this is your girl, there's something wrong with her. She's passed out."

I race into the bathroom and see feet poking out from under a stall door. I pull it open, and there's Bea. She's facedown with her hips up off the ground like she went to her knees first, then fell forward. I turn to the woman and see there are several others peering in on us. "Can someone run out and look for security? We need to get her to the hospital."

"Of course," says one bystander before she races out the door.

I look down at Bea and pick up her hand. It's so cold. "Bea, sweetheart, you're going to be okay."

In minutes, two security guards enter the bathroom. "What happened here?" asks one of them.

"She passed out."

"Is she drunk?" asks the other one. "If so, we'll have to call—"

"No, dumbass. My wife works here. She's not drunk. She's got the flu. She got sick a few minutes ago and came in here. When she didn't come out, I ask her"—I point to the nice woman—"to come in and check on her. Now, are you going to call for medical assistance, or do I need to carry her to the hospital myself?" *Jesus.*

"Ed?" Bea's eyes have fluttered open. "What's going on?"

She tries to sit up, but I place my palm on her shoulder to hold her in place. "You passed out, baby. Sit tight. We're getting help."

CHAPTER TWENTY-NINE

BEA

I feel myself being lifted off the ground onto a gurney. The movement makes me feel like I'm going to get sick again. I look over and see my stuff on the floor. "My laptop."

"I've got it, Bea," says the guy I married a month ago. I watch as he bends over and picks up my purse, notebook, and my laptop.

"Thanks."

"Miss?" asks the paramedic. "We're ready to transport. Do you have a hospital preference?"

Before I can answer, Ed pipes in, "Take my wife to the closest hospital."

I interrupt. "University of Chicago Medical Center." It's nearby, and it's where my OB/GYN works. I look at Ed who is frowning. "It's close."

"Fine." He turns to the medics. "Can I ride with her?"

The medic nods. As they roll me out, Ed keeps hold of my hand while clutching my belongings under his other arm. The ride on the gurney is a roller coaster. We've weaved around corners and gone over what feels like giant speed bumps. It's so jostling, a wave of nausea hits me. "I'm going to be sick," I say, attempting to sit up.

Before I know it, the gurney has stopped and Ed's holding a garbage can up to the edge next to me. I lean over, but nothing happens. When my stomach settles somewhat, I turn to the medics. "Can you slow down? This carnival ride is making me sick."

"Sure. Sorry," mutters one of the medics.

AT THE HOSPITAL, I'm whisked through the emergency unit into a small, semiprivate room with a curtain for a door. Ed's pulled the lone chair up to my bed. He's still holding my hand, rubbing circles in my palm and wrist. It's soothing. I should pull my hand away from him and tell him to leave, but I don't want to. I want him here.

Only ten minutes in and they've already inserted a port thing in my arm for IV fluids, but they haven't started anything yet. I'm not sure when a doctor will be in, but I hope soon. A nurse steps in to take my vitals. When she's got my pulse and blood pressure, she jots the numbers down on my chart. She asks me some questions, which I answer the best I can. I also tell her that my primary doctor is Dr. Jargon. I don't mention she's my baby doctor. I'm keeping that information to myself for now. Honestly, I have no idea how I'm going to get out of here without Ed finding out about the baby. Maybe that's the way it's supposed to be.

"Bea?"

I turn to look at Ed. "Yeah?"

"I'm sorry."

For what? There are so many things. "For what?"

"Everything."

"Wow, that covers a lot of territory, Ed. Something tells me you're not sorry for *everything*. I bet there are a few things in there that you're not sorry about. The problem is, I don't care to find out what those things are. I'm not sure I can handle what those things are."

"I get that. I don't blame you."

"Oh, that's big of you." I pull my hand away from his and slide it under the flimsy blanket that's supposed to keep me warm. It doesn't. I know I'm grumpy, and I know I promised Sarah that I'd give him a chance, but this situation wasn't of Ed's making. He just happened to be there when I passed out. He didn't come to me wanting another chance. This is just Ed doing what he thinks is right. I shouldn't fault him for that. He did that when his mom died; I suspect it's a natural response for him. It just doesn't change the fact that he's not here because he wants to be; he's here by accident.

"I deserve that."

"And more." I roll to my side facing away from him. I can't look at him. He looks so worried with his furrowed brow and concerned blue eyes.

"Bea?"

Before he can say another word, a man in a white coat steps into the room. "Miss Yousef."

"It's Flynn. Mrs. Flynn," corrects Ed.

I roll my eyes as I move to lie onto my back. "Beatrice."

"Beatrice. I'm Dr. Smart. How are you feeling now?"

"Better. When can I go home?"

"Not so fast." He chuckles. "Let's get to the bottom of your troubles." He reaches out and presses the skin on my forearm between his fingers. "You may be dehydrated. I'd like to start you on some fluids."

"Fine."

"What about that nausea? Your paperwork here says you

were ill at the hockey game. Have you been showing flu-like symptoms?"

"Um." I look over at Ed and then at the doctor. "Well—" I'm interrupted, *thank God*, when another person steps into my tiny cubicle. "Dr. Jargon?" Okay, maybe I'm not relieved. Ed's going to find out. It's inevitable now.

"Hey there, Beatrice. I got a call that you were here. What's going on?" She turns to the ER doc. "Good evening, Dr. Smart."

"She your patient?"

"She is."

"Well, now it all makes sense."

Ed sits up straight in his chair. "What makes sense?"

"Dr. Jargon is one of our best OB/GYNs." He turns to me. "Your pregnancy is probably the culprit here." Looking at my other doctor for a split second, Dr. Smart continues, "I'm still concerned about dehydration, Dr. Jargon."

I watch, like it's in slow motion, as Ed turns to face me. "Pregnant?"

I ignore him and focus all of my attention on the doctors in the room.

"She's had a tough first month. It's a concern for such a high-risk pregnancy." Dr. Jargon turns to me. "Right, Bea?" Her eyes move over to Ed as she raises her hand. "Dr. Jargon. You must be the baby-daddy?"

"Ed. Ed Flynn, and yeah, I suppose I am."

I turn to him. "You suppose?" I ask angrily. "Who else would it be, *husband*?" Okay, I've had it. I've kept it together, I've endured all of his wishy-washy, pussy-like tendencies since the day I met him. But this takes the cake. "Get out." Told you I was crabby.

"Huh?" he asks, looking shocked.

"I. Said. Get. Out." I raise my hand and point. "I planned on doing this alone, and that hasn't changed."

CHAPTER 29

"Bea. Now, wait."

"I'm. Done. I'm done waiting!" I shout. "Get out of my room." I feel nausea sweep up so fast I have to roll to the side of the bed, hoping there's a trash can nearby. God, I'm sick of puking in trash cans.

"Bea?" asks Dr. Jargon. She rushes to my side to hand me a bedpan. She turns to the ER doc. "Dr. Smart, let's get her started on fluids and some anti-nausea meds."

Dr. Smart steps out of the room and leaves the three of us alone. "Look, Ed... is it?" He nods. "The last thing she needs is someone upsetting her. Maybe it'd be best if you stayed in the waiting area until I've run some tests." She turns to me. "Bea? Do you want us to call anyone for you?"

"No."

"I already called her mom."

"My mom?" *Fluck!* "How do you know my mom's number?"

"She gave it to me before I went to Vegas. I sent her a text letting her know you were safe and sound."

"Just freaking great," Bea mutters. "I didn't want them to know. I didn't want *you* to know."

"What? Why not?"

"Oh. My. God." I run my hands over my face. "Ed, I need for you to leave, okay."

"I'll go out to the waiting area, but I'm not leaving."

"Fine. Whatever."

I watch him stand up. He looks down at me but doesn't smile. He doesn't look mad or glad or sad. It's just nothing. Stoic. Staid. The minute he steps out of the room and the curtain falls closed, I start to blubber. I've lost him now. I've pushed him away. I'm not only going to lose my sweet baby, I'm losing the man I'm supposed to be with forever.

"Bea?" Dr. Jargon places her hand on my shoulder. "Beatrice, calm down." She says it so softly I barely hear her.

"I c-can't." I've been holding it in for a month. It needs to come out.

"Do you want me to get him back in here?"

"No! I need to do this alone."

"Bea? Honey?" I look up and see my mom peeking in the room.

"Mom?" When Dad steps in behind her, I reach for the bedpan. "Daddy?"

"Honey, what's going on?" Mom rushes over and wraps her arms around me. I keep right on sobbing. "Oh, honey. I was so worried when Ed called and said you were taken to the hospital with the flu. He said you fainted."

"I d-did, but it's n-not the flu."

"It's not?" Dad asks as he moves up to the other side of my bed.

"No, Daddy. I'm... I'm p-p-pregnant."

Dad's face turns the brightest red I've ever seen. "Is it Ed's?"

I nod.

"Where has he been? He hasn't been around for a month. He just abandoned you, didn't he? I'm going to kill that son of a bitch." He turns to step out of the room, but I call him back.

"Dad, no. He didn't know. He found out five minutes ago," I say, sniffling.

"It doesn't matter. He's been the worst boyfriend you've ever had, Bea. And you've had some terrible boyfriends."

"I know, Daddy. But he's not my boyfriend."

"Well, thank God for that."

I see relief wash over my dad's face. That's going to change when I add, "He's not my boyfriend, Dad. He's my husband."

CHAPTER THIRTY

ED

When I see Mr. Yousef step out of the emergency ward, I give him a small smile. That is until I see his face. Jacob Yousef looks fucking pissed.

"You!" he points at me.

Yep. He's pissed.

"I'm going to kick your ass, son."

"Kick my ass?" I'd like to see that.

He steps in front of me, so close I can feel his breath on my neck. "You married my daughter, knocked her up, and then left her in Vegas?" He shouts so loud everyone is now focused on us.

"It's not what you think."

"Oh, yeah? You didn't marry my daughter, then leave her alone in a hotel room in Vegas?"

"Yes, but—"

"You didn't contact her in all this time?"

"No, but—"

"I'd like to have a word with your father. I'd like to ask him how he could raise such an irresponsible man."

"Hey, now that's uncalled for." No one is more responsible than me.

"Really? It's uncalled for?" He steps back. "I don't think it is. Do you want to know what I think is uncalled for?" He pauses. I remain silent. He's going to tell me even if I don't want to hear it. "What's uncalled for is for a thirty-year-old man to meet a girl like my precious Bea and make her cry six times in the first two weeks of knowing her."

"I—"

"Shh, let me finish. What's uncalled for is for the same man to chase her to Las Vegas where she was interviewing for a new job, so she could get away from *you,* by the way."

A job interview? "To get away from me?"

"That's right. But then you got her drunk and drug her to a chapel to get married." I watch as Jacob paces. "But the worst part of this is that you didn't use protection." He looks up, blinking. Softly, he adds, "She shouldn't have gotten pregnant, Ed. They said she'd never get pregnant. But now that she is, it's dangerous. She can't carry a baby full-term."

"What do you mean?"

Jacob runs his hands through his receding hairline. "Not a surprise she didn't say anything." Sighing, he walks back to me. "She has a malformed uterus. The odds of her getting pregnant were slim to none. But now that she is pregnant, the odds of her carrying a child full-term are extremely low. She'll most likely miscarry."

"Miscarry?" *She's going to miscarry our baby?* "What odds?"

"Excuse me?"

"What are the odds?"

"Low. Less than 50 percent. You'll have to ask her doctor."

I turn and race back toward the emergency ward.

"Hey," I hear behind me. "I'm not done talking to you."

"Later." I race through the door and down the long corridor to Bea's room. When I get there, Dr. Jargon is outside. "I didn't know."

She looks up at me, arching her brow.

"About any of it. I didn't know she was pregnant. I didn't know about her uterus thing. She told me she couldn't get pregnant. I assumed she meant she was on birth control. None of that matters now. I need to know what we need to do to give her the best chance of carrying our baby full-term."

"The odds are not—"

"I know the odds. What I need to know is what I can do to give her—us—the best odds."

She nods. "Let's get her through this first. She's staying the night. I want to give her more fluids and make sure she's no longer dehydrated. We can talk in the morning. Sound good?"

"Yeah." I turn to open the curtain.

"Ed...."

I know she's going to ask me to stay out of Bea's room, but that's not happening. "I'm going in there, Doctor. She's my wife, and I'm going to take care of her *and* the baby."

"Don't upset her."

"I won't." I hope I won't. "I'll try not to." Hey, I'm being honest.

CHAPTER THIRTY-ONE

BEA

When Ed enters my room again, I want to roll my eyes, but when I see his face, all I can do is blink. He knows. My dad must have told him.

"Bea, I'm going to step out and find your father. I'll be back in a bit, okay?"

I almost forgot my mom was here. "Okay," I whisper. I wipe wetness from my face and nose with the back of my hand and stare at him.

"Bea," he says softly as he approaches my bed. "Will you let me say something?"

I nod and sniffle.

"I'm sorry. I've been a dick to you since the first day we met."

I nod. Why sugarcoat things? He's right.

"I want to explain everything to you, and I will, just not right this second. Tonight... at the hockey game, I was hoping I'd see you." Ed pauses as he pulls the chair up to the side of the bed. "I didn't think going to your house was the best idea. Your dad... well, he's not fond of me. I don't blame him."

I nod. "Yeah, you're on his shit list."

"I know. He didn't hold back out there. He threatened to kick my ass." Ed chuckles.

"Don't underestimate him."

Ed smirks. "Okay, I won't. Anyway, I was hoping I'd see you tonight. I didn't have a plan. I didn't know what I was going to do when and if I saw you. I had something for you, but I wasn't even sure I was going to give it to you. When you handed me those annulment papers, I didn't think you would hear me out." He reaches into the front pocket of his jeans and pulls out a tiny bundle wrapped in what looks like toilet tissue. Taking his time, he unwraps the small item. Using his left hand, he pulls something out of the fluff. It's then I see his ring. He's wearing his wedding ring? I wasn't wearing mine. I stopped wearing my band after that disastrous brunch.

"Ed? What?"

"I took the ugly yellow ring you sent me and got you this one instead." He holds it out in front of me. I blink. "Are those daisies?" I squeak.

"Yeah. When I saw this, I thought of the day we went to Shedd Aquarium. Remember? It was our first date. You had daisies in your hair."

"Yeah, I remember." The ring is so pretty. There are diamond daisies with yellow centers that go around the band. It looks like there are seven of them.

"This ring reminds me of you, not only because of that day but because they seem like happy flowers to me. Daisies represent your free spirit."

"Actually, daisies symbolize innocence and purity. Oh, and in Norse mythology, the daisy is Freya's sacred flower. Freya is the goddess of love, beauty, and fertility, and as such, the daisy came to symbolize childbirth, motherhood, and new beginnings. Daisies are sometimes given to congratulate new mothers."

Ed starts to chuckle, but it quickly turns into a full-blown laugh. His head is thrown back. He's laughing really, really hard. I'd call it a fit of giggles if it were me doing it. I'm not sure what you call it when a guy does it.

"What's so funny?"

When he finally stops laughing, he stands up and leans over me. "You're funny, baby." He moves closer, close enough for our lips to touch. Whispering softly, he adds, "I love you, Beatrice, so much it hurts. I'm so fucking sorry I waited until all of this happened to tell you. The last month has been utter hell without you. I can't explain the reason I left you in Las Vegas, because I don't have one. I think I just freaked out. Then, I was too ashamed of myself to see you. I knew you probably hated my guts. I didn't want to see how I made you feel." He sits back in his chair but leans toward me. "When my mom died—"

"I know. Sarah told me."

He rolls his eyes. "What did Sarah tell you?"

"Everything." I recount to him the story that Sarah told me in the car that day. "So, that's why all of this today concerns me."

"It concerns you?"

"Yes. I'm concerned about the reason you're doing this now. I don't think you can help yourself. You see a problem, and you think you can fix it. But the real reason is—" She looks up at the ceiling. "—I'm not sure I can trust you. My heart can't take another disappearing act."

"I know. The only thing I can give is my word. As for the reason? It's true, I like to fix things; I feel a need to take care of and protect the people I love. I'm not going to apologize for that. I'm also not going to lie and tell you I'm not energized by the notion that I have two more people to protect and love."

"Two more people?"

"You and the baby."

"Ed, don't." I place my hand on my stomach. "The odds—"

"I know the odds. I'm not afraid of those odds. Tomorrow,

your doctor is going to talk to us, *both of us*, to tell us ways we can give our baby the best chance possible. I'll do anything and everything I can to make that happen as long as you're both safe."

"Oh, Ed… I already love this baby so much. What if I lose it?" His arms slide beneath my shoulders and the warmth of his chest presses to mine. I wrap my arms around his neck and hold tight.

"I know, baby. I know. Just give me another chance, Bea. Will you do that?" When I hear him sniffle in my ear, I pull back and see Ed is crying. Life is really messed up. How can I be so happy and be so worried at the same time? Sometimes life is a real bitch.

I sigh as I try to get myself under control. "Yes, I'll give you another chance."

CHAPTER THIRTY-TWO

ED

Thank *fuck.* "She's giving me another chance," I say as I make my way out to the waiting area. It's time for an honest discussion with Jacob and Genie. Then I'm going to have one of those with my dad. I've kept him in the dark for too long. He knows about Bea, he met her at the Flynn party, but I haven't told him anything beyond that. As I walk down the corridor, I can't help but smile. I never would have thought in a million years I'd be praying for a woman to give me the chance to prove I'm worthy of her, let alone someone quirky like Bea.

Truthfully, I've been a stubborn, arrogant ass. I just hope I'm over all of that. I fear that I may try to talk myself out of having her in my life. What if she loses the baby, God forbid? Then what? I wanted her back even before I found out about our child, so that shouldn't change. I know all of my issues stem from the death of my mom. Maybe acknowledging that loss, and how it has undermined my happiness all these years, will help me now.

In the waiting area, I don't see Genie and Jacob right away. Then I spot them sitting side by side in a corner. Genie is leaning in; I can see her lips moving. As I get closer, Jacob looks in my direction and Genie follows suit. Jacob still looks angry, while Genie just looks worried. "Can I talk to you two for a minute?"

Jacob says nothing; he only nods.

I reach for a chair and pull it in front of them. I start right in. "Look, I know I've screwed up with Bea and with you."

Jacob nods.

"There are things in my past that have sort of messed with my views on life and love."

"You mean about your mom?" asks Genie. Of course Bea told her.

"Yes. About my mom, mostly. My feelings for Bea have been complicated. I've never been in love before. Hell, I've never even had a girlfriend before. So, when I woke up in Las Vegas with a ring on my finger and a marriage license in my wallet, I freaked out."

"How do you think Bea felt that morning? Huh?" asks Jacob angrily.

"I know I hurt her. But that ends now."

"Oh?" asks Genie, sounding a little surprised.

"Yes, and here's what's going to happen."

As I talk, I can't help wanting to laugh at Jacob and Genie's facial expressions. I'm not sure if or when Jacob will ever stop scowling at me. Genie looks like she wants to cry—happy tears, I hope. "We're meeting with her OB doctor in the morning. She's going to give us the rundown on the dos and don'ts for high-risk pregnancies. After that, I'm taking Bea home."

"Okay, I'll get her room ready," says Genie nervously.

Softly, I say, "No, Genie. I'm taking her to *my* home."

"The hell you are!"

"Jacob, she's my wife."

"Oh, so now she's your wife? Where were you four weeks ago?"

"I know you're upset with me. I hope, in time, you'll forgive me. Bea has already agreed to give me another chance. If she can do it, I hope you can too."

"Well, I—"

"We will. Of course we will, Eduardo," Genie interrupts.

I chuckle. I haven't been called "'Eduardo" for weeks and weeks. "Good. Thank you, Genie. May I tell you the rest of the plan?"

Genie smiles and nods while Jacob still scowls. After a while, he joins in on the conversation. The plan is set. I'm staying the night at the hospital with Bea. In the morning, Jacob and Genie will return so we can all talk to Dr. Jargon together. It's best Bea has her entire support system in place for the weeks ahead.

After that, I'll take Bea to my house. My brothers, Ethan and Ernie, will head over to the Yousef's to get Bea's things that she'll need right away. We'll get the rest in the next week. Genie will help pack up what she needs.

"What does Bea think about all of this?" asks Jacob with his arms crossed in front of his chest.

"She's fine with it. Okay, she doesn't know about it yet. I'll speak with her when I get back to the room. My dad is coming by in the next half hour. I'd love for you to meet him. I think you'll find he's a stand-up man. Rest assured, Jacob, he'll want to kick my ass too when he hears about all of this." I chuckle.

"I'd hope so," he grumbles. "Let us talk to her about the living situation first. Will you do that?"

I nod. I'd like to be the one to talk, but it looks like this is important to Jacob. "Would you two like to go back to the room now? I'm going to get Bea some clear soda and some crackers. I'll meet you back there."

"Fine."

"We'll see you soon, honey," says Genie softly.

Thank goodness I've got one of them on my side. I'll have to work my ass off to make Jacob see I mean what I say.

CHAPTER THIRTY-THREE

BEA

"He said what?" I screech.

"He said you're moving in with him."

"No, I—"

"Beatrice, he's your husband. It's time for you to see if this thing with you two will work."

"But, Mom," I whimper. "I'm not ready to move out. I love living with you guys." I look up and see a tear in my father's eye. Of course, Mom is sobbing. She cries more than I do.

"Bea? Your mom is right. You should try it out. If you don't like it there, you can move home. But, if you want to try to make things work with him, you need to give this a go. No matter what happens, Bea, you have our support and you always have a home with us. We just want you to be happy and healthy."

"Daddy?" I sob.

My dad walks over to the bed and pushes a stray piece of hair from my face. "Angel, you know I love you more than life itself. I'd never make you do something you don't want to do. But I think Ed is sincere. Sure, I want to beat him to a pulp, but I think he'll do everything he can to care for you and my grandchild. We'll help any way we can. I suspect your mom will be over every day while Ed's at work. Right, Genie?"

"Oh, yes. We'll have so much fun. We'll watch movies. We can watch YouVideo, or whatever it's called, to learn how to knit. I've always wanted to learn how to knit. We can make a blanket or two for the baby. Oh!" She claps excitedly. "We can use the internet to buy things for the baby's room."

"But, Mom, what if—"

"Now, now. Let's think positively. If you were able to get pregnant, you can carry this baby all the way. I know you can. I can't wait to see what a beautiful baby you made with that hunk. With your personality, beautiful face, and hair and his, well, his everything...."

I giggle. "He is a hunk, isn't he?"

"He certainly is."

"He certainly is what?" asks Ed as he walks back into my tiny room. He's holding a plastic bottle with clear soda in one hand and several small packages of crackers in the other.

"No crackers." My stomach rolls just looking at them. "The soda pop sounds good though."

"We told her," deadpans my dad.

"And?"

"And I wish you'd talked to me first. I hope you don't think you're going to boss me around all the time. You're not the boss of me, Ed Flynn. You're also not going to steamroll me whenever you think you aren't getting your way. I've got my own life and interests."

"Well, *Mrs. Flynn*, I promise you I'll do my best not to boss you around. However, you're a very stubborn woman, so you may have to follow orders now and then."

"Follow orders?" I spit. "Ugh, this is never going to work." I cross my arms over my chest.

"It's going to work. And do you want to know why?" asks Ed.

"No."

Ed chuckles. "Well, I'm going to tell you anyway. It's going to work because, from the minute we met, there was something between us."

I blink at him. Is he telling the truth? "What do you mean?" I see Mom and Dad step out of the room. Probably for the best.

Ed steps up to my bed and leans over until his lips are an inch from mine, whispering, "The minute you put your hands on me, it was like you sent an electric charge through me."

I gasp. "You felt that?"

"I did. I was just too dense to know what it meant. And when we fucked"—his whisper turns husky—"it was like I was being electrocuted."

I gasp again. "I know."

"I'm starting to believe in fate or kismet, baby."

"Me too." I lean forward just enough to touch my lips to his.

"I love you, Bea."

"I love you more."

"Not possible."

CHAPTER THIRTY-FOUR

ED

At eight o'clock the next morning, Dr. Jargon and another OB specialist sit down with the four of us to go over the ins and outs of high-risk pregnancy. Bea is taking notes even though she'd already gotten some of this information at her first appointment.

Here's what we learned:

1. *Eat healthy. No drinking. No smoking. (Duh.)*
2. *Take prenatal vitamins and folic acid.*
3. *Reduce stress.*
4. *No strenuous activities or working out excessively. (Yay!)*
5. *Rely on your partner for support and ice cream. ;)*
6. *Don't google about your pregnancy. (See number 3)*
7. *Get lots of sleep. Drink lots of water.*
8. *Stay off your feet as much as possible.*
9. *Work less, if possible.*
10. *Talk to your baby. He or she loves hearing your voice already.*

We talked about the frequency of our doctor visits. Normally, a pregnant woman would see her doctor once per month. Since Bea is so worried, Dr. Jargon wants to see her every two weeks. That's not a problem. I can leave work whenever I need to. The doctor also said we'll be able to have an ultrasound at her next visit.

After the doctors leave, the four of us put our heads together to map out our plan. While I'd love for her to quit her job with the Blackhawks, she refuses. We compromise, though. She doesn't actually have to go to the games. She can get the game film sent to her so she can analyze it from home. I think Bea's pretty disappointed about that. She'll live.

The three of them already decided Genie would stay with Bea during the day most days. I'm sure they won't spend every single day together, will they? When I asked Beatrice about that, she said, "Uh, yeah. Why wouldn't we?"

"No reason. If it makes you happy...."

"She'll cook for us while she's there."

Well, hell yeah. "In that case, maybe she should move in too."

That made Bea giggle. Such a cute, tinkling sound. "Dad would miss her."

"You're probably right. If you went to live somewhere else, I'd miss you too."

"How do you know? You've never lived with me. You'll probably pull your hair out. I'm not easy to live with."

"Neither am I."

"Well, that's not a surprise. We'll just have to do our best." She rests her palm on her stomach as she says that. I place mine on top of hers.

"We'll do our best."

CHAPTER 34

OH, holy hell. Bea snores—loudly, like a bear hibernating in a cave. I've never heard anything like it. I thought it was cute at first, but after a week of trying to sleep next to her, I decide I need noise-canceling earplugs. As I lie awake in bed next to her, I pick up my iPad and open my browser to the Amazon website, typing "Noise-canceling earplugs."

"Of course they have some." I chuckle when I see the first item listed. "Eargasm High Fidelity Earplugs." Those are recommended for loud concerts. I turn to look at my lovely wife. She's certainly loud enough. Further down the list, I find *Lullies*, earplugs for sleeping. I order three pairs of those and set my iPad down.

I roll over and bring my arm over her, placing my hand on her stomach. As I scoot close enough for our bodies to touch, I glance at her nightstand. Where there used to be a lamp is now a furry lump. That's right, Mr. Barnabus Nibblesworth is now a fixture in my—no, *our* bedroom. As off-putting as the former cat is as he stares back at me with one glass eye, (I don't know where his other one is.) I'm going to have to get used to it. There's no way I'd ask her to move it. I mean, she talks to the damn thing. I caught her holding it as she read on her e-reader last night. I listened for a minute or two and couldn't help but laugh when I figured out what she was reading: The Lion King. I chuckle again just thinking about it. Damn, she's funny. Settled into my spot spooning my wife, I start to doze. It's no wonder, I'm so tired that even Snorezilla won't keep me awake.

SITTING at my kitchen island the next morning, I add to my grocery list: steak and boneless chicken breasts. We're having a dinner party with my immediate family, wives, and Bea's parents tomorrow night, so I've got to stop at the store tonight.

It's the first time they'll all be together. I hope they all get along. It'll make Bea happy, and that's all that matters.

I read through the list aloud. "Rolls, steak, chicken, salad, dressing, butter, wine, beer, and potatoes."

When I'm finished talking to myself, Bea asks, "This first week has been okay. Don't you think?" I look up and watch in awe as she makes my lunch, pressing dill pickles onto my peanut butter sandwich. *I'm not eating that.*

"Did you hear me?"

"Huh?"

"Geesh, you never listen." She slams the peanut butter jar down onto the counter.

I heard her. I was just distracted by the sandwich. I stand up from the stool I was sitting on and walk around our kitchen island. Sliding my hands around her waist, I pull her back against me. "I heard you, babe. I think things are going really well. As soon as my snore-proof earplugs get here, it'll be perfect."

She slaps my arm. "Stop it. I don't snore."

"Uh, yeah, you do. Like a freight train."

"Well, I prefer to call it purring."

"Oh, yeah? That makes it sound cute. Your snoring is *not* cute."

When she doesn't respond with a witty comeback, I peek down at her. When she sniffles, I know I went too far. "I love your noises, babe. I especially love having you in my bed every night." I put my hands on her arms and turn her to face me. Bending at the knees, I get down to her eye level. Hers are wet and sparkling.

"I'm sorry I snore. I really didn't know." She sniffles.

"Baby, I was just teasing. I sleep great. Actually, it's the best sleep I've had in well over a month."

"It is?" she asks, looking up at me. "You promise?"

"I promise."

"Well, did you know snoring is a common condition where noise is created by the vibrations at the back of one's throat while they're asleep? It happens when the air through the mouth or nose is blocked. It can be blocked through the nasal airways, from having poor muscle tone in the throat and tongue, or from having hefty throat tissue. Once you're asleep, the muscles in your tongue, throat, and roof of your mouth become relaxed and tend to vibrate."

She's smiling up at me with her pretty pink lips. I chuckle. "I love your trivia. I've learned so much from you."

"Hey, are you teasing me again?"

"No way." I lean down and kiss those sweet lips. I sweep my tongue over her full bottom lip and smile against her mouth. As I nibble on her top lip, she opens her mouth to deepen this kiss. God, I want her so badly. I spend the entire time we're home together with a hard-on, but we can't have sex. The doctor said it'd be okay early in the pregnancy, but I'm not going to risk it just to get my rocks off. We'll have plenty of sex after the baby comes. As I do my best to take my mind off my dick, I feel her hand on said dick. "Bea."

"Shh, I know we can't do 'it.' But I can still touch you, right?"

Her fingers grip either side of me through my pants, and I moan. "Oh, fuck. Yeah." I reach down and quickly unbuckle my belt, unbutton my jeans, and practically tear the zipper off. Pushing my jeans down to midthigh, Bea gasps when my cock springs out, hard as stone. "Wrap that little hand around my cock, sweetheart." She licks her palm and grasps me at the base. "Oh, fuck." With a grip I didn't expect, she brings her hand up, running her thumb over the leaking tip. "Yeah, Bea. Don't stop."

"I won't. Tell me how good I am at this."

"You're the fucking best. The best I've ever had, baby."

"You like this?" She starts to pump me faster.

"Yes, fuck yes."

When she suddenly stops, I look down at her hand then at her face. "Tell me I don't snore."

I throw my head back and laugh so loud my kitchen vibrates. "You purr, baby, like the sweetest fucking kitten in the world."

"That's what I thought."

EPILOGUE

ED: TWENTY-NINE WEEKS LATER.

When my phone rings at the jobsite, I quickly look at the name on the screen—Genie.

"Ed?"

"Genie? Is everything okay?"

"Bea started bleeding." She sniffles into the phone.

"Where is she?"

"She's here. I called an ambulance. They'll be here any minute."

"I'm close to the hospital." The house I'm working on is only a mile from the University of Chicago Medical Center. "I'll meet you there. Can I talk to her?"

Without another word, I hear shuffling noises on the other end. "Hello?"

God, her voice... I can tell she's scared. "Baby, it's going to be fine. You're at thirty-four weeks. You did amazing. The doc said if you could make it to thirty-four—"

"She said thirty-five would be better," she says, her voice quivering.

"Yeah, but thirty-four is fucking awesome. You remember what Dr. J said? If we can get to thirty-four weeks, our little girl will have a 99 percent chance everything will be fine. That's as good as 100 percent if you ask me."

"I guess."

"You did so good, angel. I'm so proud of you." When she sobs again, I nearly lose my shit. "You can do this. I'll be at the hospital waiting for you. You've got this."

"*We've* got this," she says with more determination in her voice.

"*We've* got this. You've got an entire team behind you. I'll call Dad. He'll activate the phone tree. It will be a matter of minutes before U of Chicago hospital is overflowing with Flynns and Yousefs."

"Okay. Hurry. I hear the sirens."

"I'll be there waiting. It won't be long until she's here, sweetheart. She's going to look just like you."

She snorts. "God, I hope not. If she didn't get that Flynn mojo, I think I'll scream. It's only fair she looks like you guys. She had a shitty start."

I'd laugh if it weren't all true. This pregnancy has been one worry after another. Bea's been on bedrest for the last two months, so she'll be glad to be on her feet again—but only if our little peanut is okay.

"They're here. The ambulance. I'll see you soon. I love you, Ed."

"I love you too, Bea. I'll be waiting."

"YOU'RE DOING GREAT, BEA." We're having a C-section. Well, Bea is having a C-section, but I'm here with her in the operating room.

"You keep saying that, but I can't feel anything."

"You don't want to feel anything." I'm standing so I can look over the screen they have in front of Bea. "I think she's coming, Bea." My voice sounds like I'm winded. Probably because I am. I take Bea's hand in mine. "I see her leg."

"Just her leg? Why just her leg? Where's the rest of her? Oh, God. Is she okay?" Bea starts to sob. I look down at her. When we make eye contact, I smile. "She's here." I look up at our girl, our Daisy, and start to cry. It's an amazing sight to see. I've been holding my shit together for the last two hours. "She's perfect, Bea." I wipe the tears, so I can see her clearly. She's fucking perfect. She has ten fingers and ten toes. "She's tiny."

The nurse whisks her away to a scale, cleaning her up as she goes. "Mom and Dad? She's four pounds, eight ounces."

"Oh no! That's too small. She's—"

"Bea, you know that's not true." I look up at the doc. "Right, Dr. Jargon?"

"That's a good weight for thirty-four weeks," she says confidently. "She looks good, Beatrice. Try not to worry."

The nurse then says, "She's eighteen point seven two inches long."

Bea looks up at me with beautiful, wide eyes. "Wow, that's good, right, Ed?"

"It is. Oh, they're bringing her over."

I watch as the nurse brings over our newborn, setting her onto Bea's chest. It's a moment I'll never forget—when our baby meets her mommy. They're both utterly silent until Bea speaks. "Oh, Daisy. You're so, so beautiful. I'm so happy you're finally here." Daisy Rachel Flynn lets out a little whimper then a loud cry. "Oh, my goodness. Such a big noise," Bea coos.

"That's good," says Dr. Jargon. "We want her to get those lungs going. We're going to take her to NICU now. We want to make sure everything is working as it should."

"Is something wrong with her?" asks Bea, panicked.

"We talked about this, remember? If she decided to come

early, she'd need to spend a few days in Neonatal Intensive Care. It's merely a precaution with preemies. We like to err on the side of caution. I'll watch for jaundice, and I'd like to make sure she's nursing as she should. We want her to put on some weight. But try not to worry. She looks perfect, Bea. Just like Ed said."

"Okay, Dr. Jargon."

"I've still got some work to do on you, Bea. Hang tight. We'll have you in your room holding your baby before you know it."

"Okay." Bea looks up at me. "Is your dad here yet?"

"Yep. I'm pretty sure my family took up the entire surgery waiting area."

"Good." Bea squeezes her eyes shut. When she opens them, she looks at me, worry lining her face. She whispers, "Is she really going to be okay, Ed?"

"Yes. She's going to be perfect, and it's all thanks to you, Bea. Thank you so much, honey. You did everything right. I'm so proud of you. In no time, we'll all be home living happily ever after."

Bea snorts. "You're such a dork."

"A dork who believes in happily ever afters. Thanks to you." I lean down and kiss her. "I love you, Beatrice."

"I love you more."

"Not possible."

My life has changed so much in the last year, for the better. I've got a wife who is beautiful, unpredictable, and quirky. She gave me the greatest gift a man can get—a baby girl who, I hope, takes after her mom in every single way. But if she has a little bit of my mom in her, that'd be cool too.

That'd be *very* cool.

BOOKS BY KAYT MILLER

The Palmer Sisters

Lainie

Agatha

Sadie

Cortland

Keely

Violet

Molly

Standalones

The Art of the Game

The Virginia Chronicles

One of a Kind

The Portrait Painter

Game Changer

Bedhead

It's All Thanks to Santa

Farm Boy

Coming Soon: Redhead

The Flynns

Out of the Blue

Mick'sology

<u>Vested Interest</u>

The Importance of Being Ernie

The Importance of Being Kennedy's

Quirky Girl

For a complete list of Kayt's books, visit:

Kayt's Website: kaytmiller.com

ACKNOWLEDGMENTS

Thank you to Virginia from Hot Tree Editing for editing this book from start to finish.

And an extra special thank you to Becky at Hot Tree Promotions for your advice, expertise, and her positivity.

And to my beta readers. Your feedback is essential to this process. Thank you!

Many thanks and adoration to Colleen Galligan for re-designing the The Flynn series for me. She read the books twice to get them just right. Thank you, Colleen!
To reach Colleen: galligancolleen@gmail.com

<3 KM

ABOUT THE AUTHOR

Kayt grew up in the midwest surrounded by a loving family which included three brothers, one sister, and parents who always fostered her creative side.

Kayt wrote her first book when she couldn't find a story about a certain type of a woman and a specific kind of man. She called it *Game Changer* and it couldn't have been a more appropriate title. It changed her life in many ways.

Her goal, as a writer, is to write stories that relate to all of us, to make readers laugh and maybe cry sometimes. Kayt hopes her readers can escape into a fantasy, one that's actually possible. Sure, some of the stories are dubbed "Insta-love" but that's okay. She fell in love with her husband pretty damn fast and with her daughter the second I saw her. So, it's a thing, I swear.

- facebook.com/authorkaytmiller
- twitter.com/kaytmiller1
- instagram.com/kaytmiller1
- bookbub.com/profile/kayt-miller

THANK YOU!

Thank you so much for reading Bea and Ed's story! When I start a story, it begins with an outline, notes, and lots of crazy thoughts running through my head. When I actually start writing, the characters take over, leading me through the story like they're holding my hand—guiding me. The process is exciting and cathartic. With that said, I hope you enjoy the story.

If you did, please go to my website, www.kaytmiller.com, and join my newsletter so you can be the first to know what's coming up next. And...

Please, leave a review!

SNEAK PEEK: FARMBOY

Chapter 1: Isabelle

"Mm-mm-mm. They sure don't grow boys like that out east."

My friend and co-worker, Rose, and I are both staring at the same man. "Yeah, well, *he's* not the typical Iowa farm boy."

"I think you mean *man*. Farm *man*. Because there's no boy left in that." She points at his backside as he walks down the long corridor away from us.

I snicker at her words because it's what I do when I get nervous. I giggle, snicker, snort, or straight up laugh out loud. It's my coping mechanism in situations that are too awkward for me to handle. "Even when he was a teen, he looked like that." The tall, dark-haired, muscled, beautiful man in question? Nashville James Watson. But everyone just calls him Nash.

"God, Izzy, how did you not throw yourself at that man back then?" She arches her brow. "Or now. *You're* single."

"Easy. He's my brother's best friend and two years older than me." Not to mention I was *not* the kind of girl he went with. Cheerleaders and prom queens. Those were his type.

Actually, he went with one girl that fit both those bills: Ivy DeLucas.

Rose scoffs, "Two years is nothing now. I heard he's single."

"He is." And the last I knew he wasn't looking for anything serious. "I think he's playing the field."

Rose snickers. "*I'd* play in his field..."

"Shh." I giggle. See? Nerves. Whispering, I add, "Someone will hear you." And that's definitely not what we're supposed to be doing on Open House night at our school. "We're professionals." I give her my haughtiest look, nose in the air and everything. "And what about your husband? He's great looking."

"First of all, I love my sexy husband, but it doesn't hurt to look and two, nobody can hear us way back here." Our classrooms are the last two doors in the main hallway.

Rose is our Special Education teacher, and this is my first year as the Title 1 Reading teacher at Honeywell Elementary School. Heck, it's my first year of teaching, period. I just graduated last spring. I wasn't sure about coming home. I'd hoped to find something in a big city or at least a town closer to civilization but nothing panned out and believe me, I tried. Luckily, I grew up in this town and the superintendent is a friend of my folks otherwise, I'd probably be unemployed or worse, working as a waitress like I did in college. No thanks.

Truthfully, I'm torn. A small part of me is glad to be back. The other part wished I'd found a job somewhere else, somewhere nobody already knew me so I could be anyone I wanted to be. I could have been *Isabelle* but instead, I'm back and I'm still boring old Izzy Harmon.

At least I have a job in my field. That's more than I can say about some of my friends from college. It's great because I love kids and I'm looking forward to working with all these little humans. I know some of them are children of people I grew up with so that will be good, I guess. For the most part, anyway. *Think positive, Izzy.*

It *will* be good.

I'm jolted from my thoughts when I feel my body lurch forward and realize Rose must have pushed me into his path. When he looks down at me, I blush and fumble with words, "Oh." Giggle. "Hi, Nash."

"Hey." He says walking past me like he doesn't know me. The thing is, he *does* know me. He saw me practically every day for years because Nash and my brother, Isaac were best friends and as far as I know, they still are. Heck, Nash was Isaac's best man in his wedding. I know because I was there. I was a bridesmaid. I'm pretty sure he saw me there and lord knows I haven't changed *that* much. Yes. I've changed a little bit. I started taking a kick-boxing class in college and never stopped. I love to kick and punch stuff. Who knew? It helped turn my round, soft body into a curvy soft body. I have a waist. Something I never had growing up. But there are things that won't ever change thanks to heredity and that's okay. I'm embracing my body. I'm built just like my mom and I happen to think she's gorgeous. Other than that, I'm the same Izzy Harmon he used to ignore back in high school.

You know what, never mind him. I don't need to be recognized by the town's most eligible bachelor and a guy who smells better than I remember, like man and earth. Nope. I don't need him to acknowledge me even though I honestly considered him a friend, sort of. Turns out he's just as snobby and perfect as he was back then. Too good for the likes of me. I snort because, I can't help saying, "You know, if he'd gotten down off his high horse, his pedestal once in a while, maybe he would have ended up with a good woman instead of in the mess he's in right now."

"Who are you talking to?" Rose whispers as she side-eyes me.

"Nobody."

I cross my arms in front of my chest and scowl at the little angel who just stopped in front of me. As soon as I see him, I uncross my arms and bend so I'm at his level. He's got to be in first grade. "Hi there. I'm Miss Harmon."

"I know." He's not smiling. "I'm Marcus. I guess you're my new reading teacher."

"I am." I hold out my hand to shake his but that's a non-starter. "I'm anxious to get to know you."

Marcus doesn't hold back. "I liked Mrs. Hiller."

Yep, kids are honest. It's so refreshing.

"I know. Me too." I mean that. Mrs. Hiller was an elementary teacher when *I* was in elementary school. But she died last year. She won't be coming back, but I won't say that aloud because that would be rude. Unfeeling.

"Dude, Mrs. Hiller croaked."

I look up to see a boy several years older than Marcus.

"Excuse me..." I'm about to give the older boy a good talking to when a man appears. A suit wearing man. Something not as common as you'd think in my little town.

"M.J., knock that shit off." When he looks at me, he smiles. "Oh, well, hello." He holds his hand out to me. I place mine in his and stare as he slowly bends to kiss my hand. "I'm Max Lang."

"Miss Harmon," I say rather dumbfounded.

"Miss? Is that your first name?"

I blink a few times trying to figure out if this guy is serious or if he's trying to be funny. Assuming he's serious, I reply, "Izzy."

He chuckles. "Izzy." He leans in closely glancing down my shirt. "It's a pleasure."

Not for me, it isn't.

I quickly pull back and cross my arms over my chest. I knew

I shouldn't have worn a V-neck top. But, it's Open House and it's not like it's low-cut or anything. V-necks are just more flattering on me. It's like all the magazines say, highlight your best features. Draw people's attention to that area. And no, I don't mean my boobs. I'm talking about my face and hair. I don't mean to brag. I'm no Ashley Stewart, that's for sure, but I'm not a troll either. Plus, my hair is good. It's dark brown, thick, shiny, wavy, and long. I like my hair.

"These two hellions are mine." Max points to Marcus and the older boy. "My ex-wife is out of the picture." He blinks at me expectantly.

What? Am I supposed to say something? "Oh, I'm..."

And that's when I hear someone yell. I look up to see Nash looking at me. "Max." Nash says sounding a little angry. "Come on. Let's go."

Max turns to Marcus and the other boy, M.J., "Come on guys. We're leaving."

My attention is drawn back to Marcus when he shrugs, turns, then walks down the hallway following his older brother. Turning around one last time, Max looks at me and winks. "I'm sure I'll see you again, Izzy." Max then waves as he follows his kids. When he meets up with Nash, they all take off down the hallway toward the main door. "Jerk." I mutter.

"Max?" snickers Rose.

I look over to her and smile, then laugh. "No. Yes." I'm so glad I get to work with her. We've gotten to know each other quite a bit this summer. The day after I was hired, I started setting up my classroom while she was teaching summer school for extra money. We had lunch together every day and that's when I filled her in on my old life back here in Honeywell and since she's been teaching here for several years, she filled me in on school gossip, who to avoid, and who to trust. I had no idea an elementary school could be such a hotbed of drama. It's like a soap opera around here and the school year hasn't officially started yet.

www.ingramcontent.com/pod-product-compliance
Lightning Source LLC
Chambersburg PA
CBHW030323100526
44592CB00010B/541